Storytelling Activities

◄►◄►◄►◄►◄►◄►◄►◄►◄►◄►◄►◄►◄►◄►◄►◄►◄►◄►

STORYTELLING ACTIVITIES

◄►◄►◄►◄►◄►◄►◄►◄►◄►◄►◄►◄►◄►◄►◄►◄►◄►◄►

NORMA J. LIVO
University of Colorado at Denver

SANDRA A. RIETZ
Eastern Montana College

LIBRARIES UNLIMITED, INC.
Littleton, Colorado
1987

LIBRARIES UNLIMITED, INC.
P.O. Box 263
Littleton, Colorado 80160-0263

Library of Congress Cataloging-in-Publication Data

Livo, Norma J., 1929-
  Storytelling activities.

  Bibliography: p. 139
  Includes index.
  1. Story-telling.   I. Rietz, Sandra A.   II. Title.
LB1042.L54 1987   372.6'4   86-33727
ISBN 0-87287-566-0

Libraries Unlimited books are bound with Type II nonwoven material that meets and exceeds National Association of State Textbook Administrators' Type II nonwoven material specifications Class A through E.

Contents

APPENDICES

Introduction

The values of storytelling are broad and varied.

1. Storytelling provides a much needed opportunity for listeners of all ages to interact on a very personal level. Unlike storytellers, schools classify children carefully by age groups, and the media, both television and movies, seldom provide material that can be enjoyed by people of all ages. One might say that our society operates on an age-segregated model. Storytelling, however, appeals to all and brings people together for a shared experience.

2. Storytelling develops an awareness of and sensitivity to the thoughts and feelings of the listeners. As the teller looks right at the listeners, eyes meet and an interactive communication exists between them. The storyteller gets immediate feedback on how the story is being received, and the listeners gain added messages in the story from the paralinguistic actions of the storyteller. Both storyteller and listener are actively involved.

3. Storytelling stimulates the imagination and mental visualization. As the storyteller spins his or her magic, the listener creates pictures in his or her own mind of what the setting and characters look like and creates images of the story events. Every listener will "see" images that are unique and special.

4. Storytelling is an art form. The National Association for the Preservation and Perpetuation of Storytelling defines storytelling as "an art form through which a storyteller projects mental and emotional images to an audience using the spoken word, including sign language and gestures, carefully matching story content with audience needs and environment. The story sources reflect all literatures and folkloric, entertainment, and therapeutic purposes."

5. Storytelling helps us see ourselves in a cosmological sense. Both in terms of their content and their structure, stories are the metaphor by which the mythologies of groups of people transcend empiricism. The truths of the stories are about human existence, and are intended to give meaning and value to peoples' experiences. They hold out a reality that is quite aside from the lore of science, and that operates in an entirely different context—the context of mind. The stories are human knowledge and a human way of knowing. In the hands of a competent storyteller, we discover that we are all one community. We are bound together in recognition of our universal commonalities, and we are obliged to acknowledge our shared humanity.

When used in a school setting, storytelling has additional educational values. The matrix in appendix C shows how specific storytelling activities in this book support both Bloom's *Taxonomy of Educational Objectives* and the skills identified in the National Council of Teachers of English's *Essentials of English*. In addition, storytelling has other educational values.

1. Storytelling uses the oral language. This oral dimension enriches the literary experience, contributing images and emotions that escape the devices of written language and make the stories accessible to everyone. Our language comes alive when heard.

2. Storytelling helps us remember the shape of stories. The more we hear stories, the more we learn story shapes. Storytelling aids in the development of memory suprastructures.

3. Storytellers of all ages develop confidence as they gain more experience and success with telling stories. This confidence will be like the proverbial bike-riding skill—you never forget it.

4. Storytelling improves discrimination in the choice of books and stories, and fosters an increased knowledge of literature. As storytellers search for "the right stories," they are exposed to others and are continuously making critical decisions about which stories fit them and their storytelling situation.

Good stories are like gifts. The sharing of them makes special moments which will never be forgotten. Telling and listening to stories stimulates interest, emotional and language development, and the imagination. Imagination is important for all. To be able to share these experiences with others is a great gift. For further elaboration on the values of storytelling, consult *Storytelling: Process and Practice* by Norma Livo and Sandra Rietz (Littleton, Colo.: Libraries Unlimited, 1986).

There are many opportunities, after the initial hunger for storytelling has been met, to extend storytelling experiences. This might be compared to a many course gourmet meal. We eat to satisfy our basic hunger, as well as for the aesthetic quality of the food. We have found that, accompanying the current revival of storytelling, there is an increased interest in other ways to get groups involved in storytelling activities.

The activities for storytelling presented in this book can be used at home, in schools, in libraries, and at community and organizational gatherings. They can be used effectively in either formal or informal settings. Some of the ideas would be useful for group ice-breaking and getting-to-know-you activities; others have pragmatic educational applications.

The authors feel that these activities can be used by group leaders, teachers, parents, and students. With few exceptions, the activities can be used in any order. They would be appropriate for people of all ages, and, like storytelling itself, they are intended to further the development of imagination and communication.

1

Finding a Story

INTRODUCTION

This chapter covers a range of stories from the traditional to those created entirely by the storyteller. Stories from the oral tradition can be found either by listening to storytellers or finding the stories in print form. Stories can be clustered in many ways; often stories from different cultures and periods will exhibit similar characteristics, such as structure, topic, or genre.

Modern literature often borrows heavily from the style and structure of traditional literature. For instance, Jane Yolen creates stories that could be mistaken for folk stories. However, since we know she wrote them, we know they do not fit the folk category. Good stories can be found in these current literary sources.

Legends, beliefs, and superstitions about individuals, regions, institutions, and occupations are plentiful. From this folklore has sprung a wealth of stories. Some of these stories can even be located in newspapers. Appealing articles can be clipped and filed for moments when fresh story-telling ideas are needed.

We ourselves can also create new stories to tell. These stories that we make up can borrow from the folk tradition, develop from our own family's oral literature or be entirely fanciful. Life around each of us is full of stories.

No matter where we get our stories, the important thing is that we get/create stories that we enjoy telling. The best storytellers use a wide variety of material for their tellings. The activities included here demonstrate some of the possibilities for finding/making stories.

NEWSPAPER STORIES

Read as many newspapers as you can for a week to find a story that you can make into a talking story. After all, the newspapers are the history of each day. It is all there in the articles: love, bravery, tragedy, death, birth, good fortune, riches, discovery, beauty, and sadness.

Choose an article that interests you and use it to develop a story with a beginning, a middle, and an end. Remember that you need to develop the characters, set the scene and establish a problem for the main character to overcome. Share these stories with a group.

Save your newspaper article, and write up your story. Make a group book of the stories. Did anyone choose the same article to work with? If so, how were the stories alike or different?

For a variation on this activity, make copies of an article that would make an interesting story. Give these to each person in the group and have them use the article to create stories. Share these stories.

Dolphins

This account of a dolphin that saved a young boy is a good example of a newspaper article that can be used to create an entertaining story.

*Dogged dolphin stays with boy in ocean ordeal**

PERTH, Australia (UPI) — A dolphin protected an 11-year-old boy in shark-infested waters off the Cocos Islands for four hours last week after the young surfer was swept out to sea, said the boy's father.

The boy, Nick Christides, said after his rescue that the dolphin never left his side during his ordeal in waters off the islands, 800 miles southwest of Singapore in the Indian Ocean.

He had been surfing with friends in the Cocos Island Lagoon when a wave tossed him off his board, his father Tony told the West Australian News by radio telephone Friday.

The strong current dragged him out, and boats from the island couldn't find him in the rough seas.

An Air Force P-3 Orion aircraft on the island being prepared to take off for Diego Garcia in the Indian Ocean was diverted to the search and located the boy for the search boats. "Nick may never have survived if the dolphin had not stayed with him. He was very very lucky. We were sure we would never see him alive again," said Christides, who lives on the island.

He said Nick told him after the rescue that when he first saw the dolphin, "he thought it was a shark, but

*"Dogged dolphin stays with boy in ocean ordeal." 15 August 1982. Reprinted from the *Rocky Mountain News*, Denver, Colorado.

then it started blowing water and Nick knew it wasn't."

"The dolphin just stuck with him, either swimming beside him or going around in circles. He must have realized Nick was in trouble and that the boy was being pulled out by the northerly current because he just followed him and stayed with him all the time."

Nick "kept his head and didn't panic. That's what got him out of it. That and the dolphin," Christides said.

After the telling, you should invite your group to participate in discussion of the story and activities related to it. Following are questions and comments to address to the group, and related activities to suggest:

- Tell or write a story from the point of view of Nick Christides. In this first-person story tell what you (as Nick) felt and thought. How did the dolphin look? What did the dolphin do? Would you give the dolphin a name?

- Write a poem about Nick's encounter with the dolphin.

- There is a reference to Greek and Roman mythology in this article. The aircraft that located Nick was a P-3 Orion. What can you find out about Orion? (Orion was a hunter whom Diana loved but accidentally killed. He was placed in the heavens by her as a constellation.) Can you create a new story incorporating the Nick Christides incident (don't you appreciate Nick's last name?) and the story of Orion?

LITERARY STORIES

◄►◄►◄►◄►◄►◄►◄►◄►◄►◄►◄►◄►◄►◄►◄►◄►◄►◄►◄►

There are outstanding examples of literary tales that can be used for storytelling. Read stories by the following authors:

Isak Dinesen	Isaac Bashevis Singer
Jane Yolen	Edgar Allan Poe
Mark Twain	James Thurber

You may find among their stories some that are fun to learn and tell.

◄►◄►◄►◄►◄►◄►◄►◄►◄►◄►◄►◄►◄►◄►◄►◄►◄►◄►◄►

OCCUPATIONS IN FOLKTALES

◄►

Use a folklore collection by the Grimm brothers for this activity. Skim through the stories Jacob and Wilhelm collected from the German folk. What occupations do you find in these stories? There should be millers, woodcutters, or minstrels, and other examples of working folk.

Now, retell one of the stories but substitute a twentieth-century job such as astronaut, computer scientist, rock star, or geologist. How will you have to change the story to accommodate the updated occupation? What details do you need to add? Is *Star Wars* really just an updated folktale?

◄►

HEROES AND HEROINES

◄►

Ask each person to compose a story about someone he or she regards as a hero or heroine. The chosen person could be a relative, a friend, a local or national or international figure, or someone from history.

Have people share stories in groups of four. They should explain why they chose their particular hero or heroine.

◄►

SPONTANEOUS CREATIVITY

Objectives: To understand that creative thinking derives from the ability not only to look, but to see; not only to hear, but to listen; not only to imitate, but to innovate; not only to observe, but to experience the excitement of fresh perception.

Materials needed: Slips of paper with unusual character, problem, and setting ideas.

Procedure: Prepare unusual character, problem, and setting ideas. Write them on slips of paper and place them in boxes marked "Character," "Problem," "Setting." Ask the participants to take turns drawing an idea from each box and developing a spontaneous story using the selected idea.

Examples:

Character	Problem	Setting
giant	storm	in a forest
mosquito	amnesia	in the desert
anteater	need for money	up Jack's beanstalk
beaver	lost	on a horse
fairy godmother	nearsighted	in Africa

The participants themselves might also create new ideas for the categories of "Character," "Problem," and "Setting."

MIRROR, MIRROR ON THE WALL

◀▶ ◀▶ ◀▶ ◀▶ ◀▶ ◀▶ ◀▶ ◀▶ ◀▶ ◀▶ ◀▶ ◀▶ ◀▶ ◀▶ ◀▶ ◀▶

Make a drawing of the frame of a large, ornate mirror on heavy poster-board. Cut out an oval in the center so people can hold it up and put their faces in the mirror. Explain that this mirror is a magic one which will enable each person to see a scene from his or her past. As the mirror is held to each face (with the ornate side of the mirror toward the listeners), each person will explain what scene he or she sees.

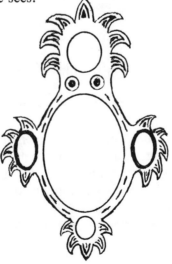

◀▶ ◀▶ ◀▶ ◀▶ ◀▶ ◀▶ ◀▶ ◀▶ ◀▶ ◀▶ ◀▶ ◀▶ ◀▶ ◀▶ ◀▶ ◀▶

HERE IS A GOOD ONE FOR YOU

◄►◄►◄►◄►◄►◄►◄►◄►◄►◄►◄►◄►◄►◄►◄►◄►◄►◄►

Divide a group of people into pairs. One person chooses a phrase or an object, and the other must create a story about it. Give each person a chance to both choose the phrase or object and to tell a story.

◄►◄►◄►◄►◄►◄►◄►◄►◄►◄►◄►◄►◄►◄►◄►◄►◄►◄►

AND THEN WHAT HAPPENED?

◄►◄►◄►◄►◄►◄►◄►◄►◄►◄►◄►◄►◄►◄►◄►◄►◄►◄►

Have everyone sit in a circle. Instruct someone to start a story, then stop, point to someone else, and say, "And then what happened?" The second person then continues the story from the point where the first teller quit. The story can continue like this until someone officially ends the story.

A variation on this activity uses a long piece of yarn with unevenly spaced knots tied in it. Roll the yarn up into a ball. Have the person starting the story hang on to the end of the yarn, and pass the ball around the circle. As the yarn ball travels, the narrator of the story changes whenever someone gets a knot; that person then takes over in the story until the next knot comes up.

◄►◄►◄►◄►◄►◄►◄►◄►◄►◄►◄►◄►◄►◄►◄►◄►◄►◄►

PASS THE STORY

◄►◄►◄►◄►◄►◄►◄►◄►◄►◄►◄►◄►◄►◄►◄►◄►◄►◄►

Seat everyone in a circle. Have one person begin telling a story. Ring a bell at random moments as a signal for the next person to continue the story. (Or when the bell interrupts, the person telling the story can pick the next teller.) Continue until the story is completed.

◄►◄►◄►◄►◄►◄►◄►◄►◄►◄►◄►◄►◄►◄►◄►◄►◄►◄►

STORYTELLING WARM-UP IDEAS

Objective: To develop the skill of inventiveness and the ability to see new relationships.

Materials needed: Cards with ideas.

Procedure: Put the following ideas on cards. Have people draw a card, work with the idea on it, and then present it to your group.

- Imagine you are an object. Be that object and tell a story from the object's point of view.

- Recall a personal experience using sensory recall. How did things/people look, smell, feel, taste? What sounds and colors were there? Was it hot or cold? Tell about it.

- What is the earliest personal experience you can remember? How old were you? Where were you? What happened?

- Create three characters. Put them in a conflict situation. Tell the story of how the conflict was resolved.

- Concentrate on observing an object for 10 minutes. Take no notes. Afterwards, write details that describe the object. (This is a good exercise for heightened awareness.)

- Compose a short story that includes an obscure word. Use the story or pun to teach that vocabulary word. A good source of ideas is *The Weighty Word Book* by Paul M. Levitt, Douglas A. Burger, and Elissa S. Guralnick (1985).

- Draw a picture or sculpt a character from a story you have heard. Be as detailed as possible.

- Use the phrase, "No I won't do it," and present it to show anger, boredom, irritation, grief, surprise, joy, fright, shyness, and slyness. Have the group guess each mood you are expressing.

- Tell the story "The Three Little Pigs" from the point of view of the wolf.

- (For two people) Tell a very simple tale to your partner. Retell your partner's story, substituting synonyms for the words used.

- (For two people) Choose a folktale and create a bare-bones version that leaves as much as possible to the imagination; tell this version to your partner. Retell your partner's story, adding the flesh back to the bare-bones story by means of beautiful language.

- (For two people) Create a story about a phrase or thing chosen by your partner.

CRAZY CRITTERS

◄►

What creatures did not get on board Noah's Ark? Create your own creature that "missed the boat." Make your invention as offbeat as possible.

Tell a story explaining why your special critter was not on board Noah's traveling zoo.

◄►

PLAYING SCHEHERAZADE

◄►

Scheherazade, the storyteller in *The Thousand and One Nights* spins nightly tales for her king. These tales are from the eleventh-century Indo-Persian period and constitute a story cycle. The cycle is in a story framework that provides context and opportunities for innumerable stories. Other examples of stories within a larger story framework concern King Arthur and the Knights of the Round Table, the Man of LaMancha, Tolkien's hobbits, Anansi the Spider, and Coyote, right up to characters in today's soap operas.

Develop a frame story that will allow for innumerable substories and creation of your own story cycle.

After you have established the frame story and characters, you have an opportunity for spontaneous group story inventions. Each person in the group could develop a story or collection of stories for this cycle. These stories, then, could be collected, illustrated, and mounted in a book for others to read.

◄►

"NO SUCH THINGS"*

◄►◄►◄►◄►◄►◄►◄►◄►◄►◄►◄►◄►◄►◄►◄►◄►◄►◄►

Using rhythmic verse, Bill Peet has created a picture book full of creatures that amuse and delight listeners and readers

> If the fancy Fandangos seem stuck-up and snooty,
> It is mostly because of their exquisite beauty.
> They're most often seen with smug smiling faces,
> By a crystal clear pond in a jungle oasis.

Each of these descriptions of fanciful creatures is accompanied by Peet's fanciful crayon illustrations. After hearing several of these verses, have the audience create their own fanciful characters and illustrate them. These creations could be bound into a group book of their own **No Such Things**.

◄►◄►◄►◄►◄►◄►◄►◄►◄►◄►◄►◄►◄►◄►◄►◄►◄►◄►

*In Peet 1983.

"BROWN BEAR, BROWN BEAR, WHAT DO YOU SEE?"*

◀▶ ◀▶ ◀▶ ◀▶ ◀▶ ◀▶ ◀▶ ◀▶ ◀▶ ◀▶ ◀▶ ◀▶ ◀▶ ◀▶ ◀▶ ◀▶ ◀▶ ◀▶

The language pattern of this story book is quickly learned by children, for whom stories like this work particularly well.

"Brown Bear, Brown Bear, What do you see?"

"I see a redbird looking at me."

Of course the next question is patterned after the question to the Brown Bear. What does the redbird see "looking at me"? And so it goes in this picture book. The illustrations are boldly colored collages and complement the text beautifully. After enjoying this book, the listeners will be ready to use the familiar pattern to create their own book. Have available a large number of cut out pictures. Each child should pick out ten pictures of things that are related (ten cars, ten vegetables, ten people, ten toys, or ten articles of clothing). Each child then pastes a picture on a page of paper and writes a personal version of the patterned question story.

Materials needed: Paper, writing implements, pictures, paste.

Variation: Have the children select and cut out their own pictures from catalogs, newspapers, and magazines.

◀▶ ◀▶ ◀▶ ◀▶ ◀▶ ◀▶ ◀▶ ◀▶ ◀▶ ◀▶ ◀▶ ◀▶ ◀▶ ◀▶ ◀▶ ◀▶ ◀▶ ◀▶

---

*In Martin 1983.

FROGERATURE

◄►

Well-known storyteller Jackie Torrence once stated firmly, "Everyone needs at least one good frog story." Since everyone needs one, the world needs more good frog stories.

Make up your own frog story. First, you might want to study existing "frogerature" literature. For froggy sources, refer to *Storytelling: Process and Practice* by Norma J. Livo and Sandra A. Rietz (Littleton, Colo.: Libraries Unlimited, 1986).

As you develop your story, consider these questions:

- What size is your frog character?
- What sounds does it make?
- How does it move?
- What is a day in the life of your frog like?
- What does your frog eat?
- What problem does your frog have?
- Where does your frog live?

If people in a group each create a frog story, these fantastic frog stories can be typed, illustrated, and made into a frog anthology for others to share.

◄►

PICK AN OBJECT, PICK ANY OBJECT

◄►

Place a variety of interesting objects on a table. Have each person select one. Divide the group into pairs, and have each explain to the other why he or she chose that object. Change the pairs two times. Each time each person must give a different reason for chosing that particular object.

After they have completed this, have the group members write a story about the object. Have them share their stories.

Did the three explanations about why they chose their object influence or help them tell and write a story?

Objects can include anything at all: feathers, shells, dry flowers and plants, a piece of jewelry, an odd piece of drift wood—anything at all.

◄►

STORY MAPPING — TO CREATE A STORY

Personal artifacts make good subjects for story invention, provided that the artifact is generic enough to lend itself to many possibilities. The best items to use are those for which you know a bit of history and which suggest a mysterious past. Use old articles of clothing that belonged to members of your family. For example, one of the author's best story stimulators is a hat, the property of an aunt who used to be in vaudeville. The hat is a flamboyant, turn-of-the-century affair, wide-brimmed, in black satin and wine-red velvet, with a collection of matching ostrich plumes sweeping rakishly over the front brim, down, and to one side. The hat, worn at a fashionable angle and held in place with a poker-sized, pearl-tipped hat pin, is quite an elegant thing. It was never worn on stage, since it was an article of regular clothing. And, because the theater company toured various cities in the northern midwest — Milwaukee, Chicago, Detroit, Duluth, Minneapolis, Bismarck — the hat probably went to all of those places. It may have spent part of its life in a trunk. It otherwise got a good view of times and places.

The hat conjures visions, which, in turn, can become stories. Children gather on the floor, around a long piece of newsprint. They and the teller, talk about the hat — who owned it, when she/they owned it, when and where she/they wore it, how she/they got it, who she/they eventually gave it to, and how the teller got it. All try the hat on and otherwise examine it closely. Before long, even first grade children are convinced that they know intimate details in the life of the hat and forget, quickly enough, that the teller is connected to it in any way. (One group of third graders decided that the hat had belonged to Al Capone's girlfriend and was valuable because it contained smuggled microfilm — an interesting mixture of history and technology. This scenario led to a series of bloody stories which read like contemporary TV dramas. And we aren't sure that TV affects thinking....) The children become engaged in a spontaneous story swap, beginning with the historical data, and ending in a mapping exercise.

As they imagine stories in which the hat plays a part (although some of them forget the hat entirely), the children begin to tell each other their stories in brief form. When a sufficient number of children have stories, but before everyone has had a chance to tell one, the teller begins the mapping. The group goes back to the beginning. The teller reminds the children that they began with the hat, and that all of their good ideas originate from it. With a felt-tipped pen the teller writes the word "hat" in a circle (a webbing) at the center of the paper. Then one child at a time traces his or her story forward from "hat" (see figure 1.1). The group webs, idea for idea, word for word, until they arrive at the key word or idea which triggered each child's story. A few questions establish that the child knows the people in his or her story, knows that will happen to them, and knows how the story will begin and end. The child has a sense of the "problem" for creating the story and a "vision," a view of the structure that it will take. The child then signs his or her name to the web at his or her key word. This procedure is repeated for each child. (See Livo and Rietz 1986, 38.)

The process sounds like a painfully long ordeal in which a separate dimension of the web must be created for each child, but this is not what happens. The only lengthy mappings occur with the first two to three children. Thereafter, the children tend to cluster about key words or along web chains leading to various key words. Once the children understand that they are to interrupt at the point in the webbing where they find their story, hands go up quickly. One by one, the children reiterate their ideas, sign their names, then retire to a corner or desk to write.

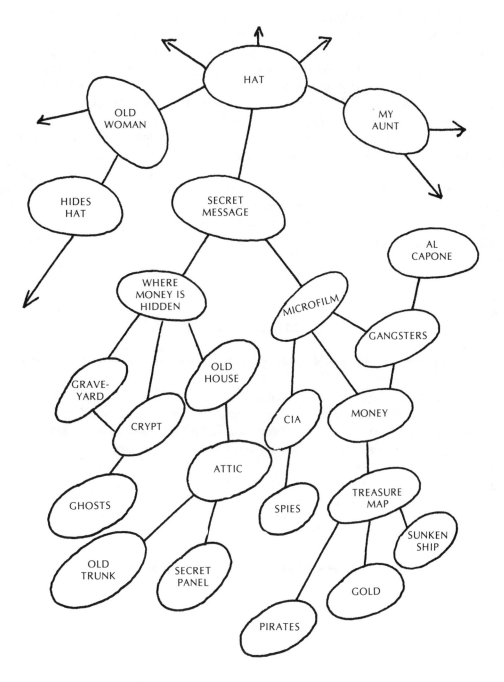

Fig. 1.1. A child's webbing.

Children who did not volunteer a story initially may now "see" one, having had the procedure demonstrated repeatedly by their classmates. The teller works with the children until even the last one has discovered a story, and the last one or two may take time.

The web can be hung; it is, by now, a mural. It can also be illustrated, with each child drawing a part of his or her story on the paper, with lines to their signatures in the web. Finally, their revised written work can also be attached to the web, a good disposition, which serves to remind the children of the steps in the writing process.

With this exercise, oral storytelling precedes making written stories and provides opportunity, during prewriting, for the student to construct a top level structure to guide the writing and to serve as a basis for the slotting of content.

For students of storytelling and practicing storytellers, the exercise might be modified somewhat. The product might be an oral story rather than a written one. Otherwise, the same webbing procedure might suffice, with each individual eventually spending several private moments constructing his or her story (perhaps making notes) for a group telling.

MAGIC HAT

◄►◄►◄►◄►◄►◄►◄►◄►◄►◄►◄►◄►◄►◄►◄►◄►◄►◄►

Place an imaginary hat on a chair or table. Tell the listeners that this hat is full of objects from a story—big things, tiny things, and amazing things. Have someone come up, take something from the Magic Hat, and pantomime how that object is used. Each person must consider not only the object but who uses it, how to use it, and when to use it. The objective of this pantomime activity is to see if each person can create an illusion and if the audience can identify the object.

If they wish, the participants could then develop the objects into an original story.

◄►◄►◄►◄►◄►◄►◄►◄►◄►◄►◄►◄►◄►◄►◄►◄►◄►◄►

GUIDED FANTASY

Use a gentling or relaxation exercise before getting into guided fantasy experiences. Then talk the listeners through the outline of a fantasy that is structured in such a way that the listeners must fill in the blanks and use their imaginations. While guiding the experience, include pauses for developing the inner imaginative thinking of the participants. The actual guided story (not including pauses) should probably last for five minutes. During this time, each listener should feel a sense of having either experienced a dream while awake, or having lived through a novel.

Within the guided fantasy, leave blanks for listeners to recall buried childhood memories and stories. Favorite places are also good to include.

A Fantasy

◄►◄►◄►◄►◄►◄►◄►◄►◄►◄►◄►◄►◄►◄►◄►◄►◄►◄►◄►

"You are about to go off on a trip. Get yourself relaxed and comfortable. Close your eyes.

Imagine you are in the place that you love most. [Pause.] Where is this place? What does it smell like? What memories do you have of this place? Why is it your favorite place? You leave this place and start out on a trip. [Pause.] Where are you going? Who and what will you see when you get there? What will you take with you for this trip? You get there and experience the most joyful experience you have ever had. [Pause.] What was that experience? What made it so joyful for you? Did others realize what was happening? What did you do after it? And now, you are being whisked up in the air by a gentle, cool breeze. [Pause.] Where does it take you? What happens when you get there? Does your story end there?

Now slowly come back to where you are now. Open your eyes."

◄►◄►◄►◄►◄►◄►◄►◄►◄►◄►◄►◄►◄►◄►◄►◄►◄►◄►◄►

You may ask for volunteers to share their stories. As people share, others may be reminded of similar thoughts. They have all, if they have concentrated, brought back warm stories from their past. Our memories are invisible cargo that we all carry with us wherever we go.

REFERENCES

Leavitt, Paul M., Douglas A. Burger, and Elissa S. Guralnick. 1985. *The Weighty Word Book.* Longmont, Colo.: Bookmakers Guild.

Livo, Norma J., and Sandra A. Rietz. 1986. *Storytelling: Process and Practice.* Littleton, Colo.: Libraries Unlimited.

Martin, Bill, Jr. 1983. *Brown Bear, Brown Bear, What Do You See?* Illustrated by Eric Carle. New York: Holt, Rinehart & Winston.

Peet, Bill. 1983. *No Such Things.* Boston: Houghton Mifflin.

2

Designing the Story

INTRODUCTION

Storytellers are able to construct (tell) stories because they have mental models for the idea of "story" (see Livo and Rietz 1986) and for specific story patterns (the manner in which specific stories are organized). Audiences, likewise, operate their mental models for "story" and stories when listening to a storytelling. Both storytellers and audiences are able to make meaning using the devices of "story" by imposing their own mental models upon a given story, or by using what they already know about how stories should work to predict the structure and operation of a given piece of material. The degree to which and the manner in which such imposition occurs in storytelling depends upon the task—the role enacted by an individual or an audience. This chapter addresses a variety of such tasks or roles, each of which specifies a different kind of prediction and/or imposition of structure upon a story.

The chapter contains a collection of activities that describe four different classifications of structural prediction or imposition. The first category, mapping, provides opportunity for an audience to map story structure before and after a storytelling. Both exercises are task awareness activities for audiences and illustrate the predicting procedures that are a part of audience inter-action with a told story. The second category, constructing, provides an activity for would-be storytellers that clarifies the role of the storyteller in "slotting" story content into story structure during telling. The third category, tailoring, extends the storyteller's role in that it suggests a variety of means by which a teller can change a story without violating its overall pattern or intent. The fourth category, predicting point of view, allows a storyteller to practice with developing story character behavior based upon an examination of point of view.

16

While this chapter certainly does not provide answers to that perennial question of the storyteller—"What shall I do with this story to invest it with oral and visual imagery?"—it gives suggestions. Storytellers are aware that the very telling of a story infuses the material with features that are the interpretive inventions of the teller. These inventions are the products of the imagination of the teller, constructed in conjunction with the teller's understanding of the story itself. The act of telling the story, then, is the imposition of the mental models of the teller on the story. The sensitive storyteller is always aware of that imposition, and is always concerned with discovering which interpretive elements suit the story and which do not.

STORY MAPPING—AFTER THE TELLING

Most people, with the usual exception of the very young child, "know" how stories work. They have learned "story" and a number of variations of story patterns inductively, from hearing stories, and hold these schema in memory as "top level" structures, or macro-structures. They "know" that "story" is a way of organizing information. They can distinguish something that is a story (storied information) from something that is not.

Once an individual "knows" story, he or she can learn to "map" a story. (The individual has already mapped stories in memory and "story" itself represents a knowledge structure that can be imposed on other stories.)

1. Story mapping exercises for prospective storytellers are very instructive, since story structure is usually not conscious memory. Beginning storytellers are more often fearful of memorizing a whole story word-for-word, and of forgetting it at a critical moment, than they are of the fact of working with an audience. Once they understand that most stories should not be memorized, they relax somewhat. They then want to know what device, if not word perfect memory, they will employ to tell a story. Such concerns lead to a discussion of story structure and of "slotting" story content into that structure during the construction of the story. People are quite relieved to discover that they can remember and tell a story more effectively by working with the macro-structure instead of at the single word level. The next question has to do with recognizing this internal structure. What, when we look for structure, are we going to find? A story mapping is a useful problem-solving tool.

2. Beginning readers can, perhaps, be equated with beginning storytellers in that they are imposing story structure on stories for purposes of comprehension. (Neither beginner is operating at a conscious level.) The more successful reader does a better job of slotting story content into an internalized top level structure. While studying literary form is not an appropriate activity for young students, construction of a story map can help beginning readers to discover the bigger shapes that govern the organization of sentences, words and sounds.

Choosing the appropriate story for mapping is important for work with groups who have never mapped a story or even made a conscious attempt to look at the top level organization of a story. The following tale is a reconstruction of a story that appeared in *The Atlantic*. In its adapted form, it is so very regular and predictable that first grade students can map it with success. Storytelling students "see" its structure instantly.

"The Farmer and His Animals"*

◄►◄►◄►◄►◄►◄►◄►◄►◄►◄►◄►◄►◄►◄►◄►◄►◄►◄►

One time there was an old man. Had a farm. Had a cow, a pig, and a turkey. Woke up one morning with a powerful cravin' for steak. Took up the axe, then. Went on out to butcher that cow.

Cow saw him a-comin'. Cow saw the axe. By the time the old man laid a-holt of the cow's collar, cow had it all figgered out. Sez, "Old man, you don't want to butcher me. I ain't nothin' but a common, ordinary cow. You butcher me, you'll git steak and ribs—nothin' more. Hit'l last you for a bit, and when it's gone, it's gone. Then you'll be sorry. If I was you, I'd butcher that pig over there. That pig's enchanted. You butcher that pig, you'll git hams and chops and bacon. But the best part is: you butcher that pig; take them pigs ears; make a purse; that purse'll be magical; hit'l fill itself with money faster n' you can git it spent, ever' day, for the rest of your life."

Old man didn't butcher the cow, then. Put up the axe. Went back up to the house to do some thinkin'. Did some thinkin'. Got done thinkin'. Took up the axe. Went on out there to butcher that pig.

Pig saw him a-comin'. Pig saw the axe. By the time the old man laid a-holt of the pig's ears, pig had it all figgered out. Sez, "Old man, you don't want to butcher me. I ain't nothin' but a common, ordinary pig. You butcher me, you'll git hams and chops and bacon, nothin' more. Hit'll last but a day, and when it's gone, it's gone. You gonna miss me. If I was you, I'd butcher that turkey over there. That turkey's enchanted. You butcher that turkey, you'll git you a fine roast. But the best part is: you butcher that turkey; take one o' them turkey legs; hang it 'round your neck on a string; hit'll be magical; hit'll protect you. Won't no harm ever come to you again for the rest of your life."

The old man didn't butcher the pig, then, Put up the axe. Went up to the house to do some thinkin'. Did some thinkin'. Got done thinkin'. Took up the axe. Went on out there to butcher that turkey.

Turkey saw him a-comin'. Turkey saw the axe. By the time the old man laid a-holt of that turkey's neck, turkey had it all figgered out. Sez, "Old man, you don't want to butcher me. I ain't nothin' but a common ordinary

---

*Adapted and retold by Sandra A. Rietz from Harris 1986, 32.

turkey—skinny, scrawny, and stringy. You butcher me, you'll git a puny roast, nothin' more. Hit'll last you half a minute. Then what you gonna do? If I was you, I'd butcher that cow over there."

Old man studied that turkey real hard, sez, "Doggoned if hit ain't another talkin' animal." Sez to the turkey, sez, "And I suppose you're gonna tell me that thet cow's enchanted, too, then!" "Why, yeeesss!," sez the turkey. "Can't you tell? That's one of the finest specimens of enchanted cow I ever saw. You butcher that cow, you'll git steak and ribs. But the best part is; you butcher that cow; you make a suitcase out of that cowhide. Ever' time you lay holt o' thet handle, you'll be magically transported anywhere on earth you want to go."

Old man didn't kill the turkey, then. Put up the axe. Went back up to the house to do some thinkin'. Did some thinkin'. Got done thinkin'. Took up the axe! Went on out there—butchered the cow, the pig and the turkey!

He ate steak and ribs; he ate hams and chops and bacon; he ate turkey roast. But the best part was … he made a suitcase out of the cowhide. He made a purse out of the pig's ears, and he hung one of them turkey legs 'round his neck on a string.

He travelled all over the world. Never did have no problems with cash flow. And no harm ever come to him ever again for the rest of his life.

◄► ◄► ◄► ◄► ◄► ◄► ◄► ◄► ◄► ◄► ◄► ◄► ◄► ◄► ◄► ◄► ◄► ◄► ◄►

While the story, as given here, is a considerable extension of the original, it is reconstructed to achieve a very high degree of regularity and predictability. This story is exceptionally conventional and very easily mapped.

While a webbing could be employed, a "box" map will do just as well. Adult storytellers can map the story by talking out its structure and drawing figures in the air. Children do a better map if allowed to crawl about on a large strip of newsprint. Figure 2.1 is a first grade version of a "box" map.

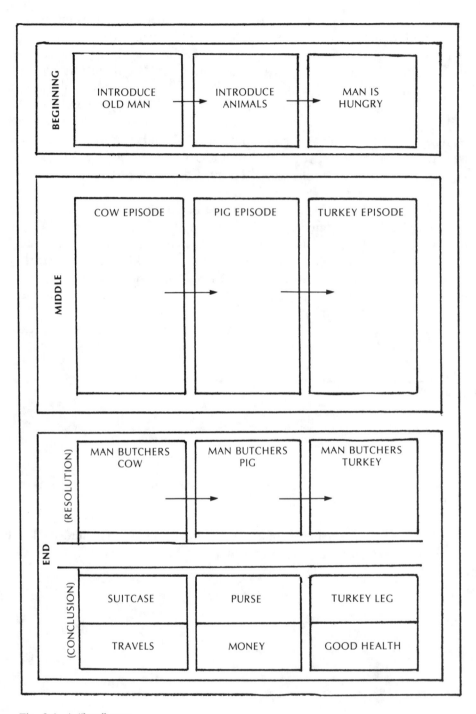

Fig. 2.1. A "box" map.

HOW DID THAT STORY GO?

Procedure: There are three stories, "Heron and the Hoopoe Bird," "Sweet Porridge," and "Old Grandfather's Corner" on the following pages. These stories could be photocopied for use. Cut each story into sections on the dotted lines. For self-checking later, mark each slip on the back to show the order of the sections. Put each story in a separate envelope.

Divide a group of participants into three groups. Give each group one of the envelopes with the cut-up story slips in it. Instruct the groups to take the slips out, and place them in the proper sequence to make story sense. When they have done this, they can either check the sequence with the numbers marked on the back, or you can give each a photocopy of the complete story to check.

This part of the activity involves the skill of sequencing and developing a familiarity with the story. It also uses predictability to establish what happened next. Each person in each group will study the story after having successfully placed it in order. Each person should learn the story to tell it. Obviously, he or she should not memorize it, but take a bare-bones story and learn its structure.

Have one person from each of the three groups form a new group. There will be someone who worked with "Heron and the Hoopoe Bird," "Sweet Porridge," and "Old Grandfather's Corner" in each of these groups. For the next assignment, each person tells to the other two people the story he or she learned in the original group. In that way each person experiences and tells one story, and each person hears two other stories.

The next step is to have each person take the original story and flesh it out. Can he or she develop the characters more, add more details to the setting, establish time clearly and come up with sounds or actions to fit the story? Suggest that the participants change the story to suit themselves. They can place it in any culture, time frame, or setting. They should feel free to elaborate on it and embellish it at will.

When it looks like people have worked their story for the next telling, have them again form groups of three. These groups could be people who worked on the same story or a mixture of stories. Each person will then tell their restoried version.

Evaluation: Have everyone compare reactions to the stories they heard concerning what worked, what didn't work, and what happened that they really liked.

"The Heron and the Hoopoe Bird"*

◄►◄►◄►◄►◄►◄►◄►◄►◄►◄►◄►◄►◄►◄►◄►◄►◄►◄►◄►

"Where do you like to feed your flocks the best?" said a man to an old cowherd. "Here, sir, where the grass is neither too rich nor too poor, or else it is no use." "Why not?" asked the man. "Do you hear that melancholy cry from the meadow there?" answered the shepherd. "That is the heron. He was once a shepherd, and so was the hoopoe bird. I will tell you the story."

— —

"The heron pastured his flocks on rich green meadows where flowers grew in abundance, so his cows became wild and unmanageable. The hoopoe drove his cattle onto high, barren hills, where the wind plays with the sand. His cows became thin and had no strength.

— —

When it was evening, and the shepherds wanted to drive their cows homewards, the heron could not get his together again. The cows were all too high-spirited and ran away from him. He called, 'Come, cows, come,' but it was no use. The cows took no notice of his calling.

— —

The hoopoe, however, could not even get his weakened cows up on their legs. 'Up, up, up,' screamed he, but it was in vain. The cows remained lying on the sand.

— —

That is the way when one has no moderation. And to this day, though they have no flocks now to watch, the heron cries, 'Come, cows, come,' and the hoopoe bird cried, 'Up, up, up,' "

◄►◄►◄►◄►◄►◄►◄►◄►◄►◄►◄►◄►◄►◄►◄►◄►◄►◄►◄►

---

*Adapted from *Grimm's Complete Fairy Tales*, n.d.

"Sweet Porridge"*

◄►

There was a poor but good little girl who lived alone with her mother, and they no longer had anything to eat. So the child went into the forest, and there an aged woman met her who knew about her sorrow, and presented her with a little pot.

— —

The old woman told the little girl that if she told the pot, "Cook, little pot, cook," it would cook sweet porridge. The pot would stop making porridge only if she told it, "Stop, little pot, stop."

— —

The girl took the pot home to her mother, and now they were freed from their hunger and ate sweet porridge as often as they chose.

— —

Once when the little girl had gone out, her mother said, "Cook, little pot, cook." As usual, the pot cooked and the mother ate till she was full. She wanted the pot to stop cooking, but did not know how to stop it.

— —

So the pot went on cooking, and the porridge rose over the edge, and still it cooked on until the kitchen and the whole house were full. The porridge moved on to the next house, and then the whole street just as if it wanted to satisfy the hunger of the whole world. There was great distress as the porridge spread but no one knew how to stop it.

— —

At last, when only one single house remained, the child came home and quickly said, "Stop, little pot, stop." It stopped cooking, and people who wished to return to the town had to eat their way back.

◄►

———————

*Adapted from *Grimm's Complete Fairy Tales*, n.d.

"Old Grandfather's Corner"*

◀▶ ◀▶ ◀▶ ◀▶ ◀▶ ◀▶ ◀▶ ◀▶ ◀▶ ◀▶ ◀▶ ◀▶ ◀▶ ◀▶ ◀▶ ◀▶ ◀▶ ◀▶ ◀▶

Once upon a time there was a very old man who lived with his son and daughter-in-law. His eyes were dim, his knees tottered under him when he walked, and he was very deaf. As he sat at the table his hand shook so that he would often spill the soup over the table cloth or onto his clothes. Sometimes he could not even keep the soup in his mouth when it got there.

— — — — — — — — — — — — — — — — — — — —

His son and daughter were so annoyed to see his actions at the table that they placed a chair for him in a corner behind a screen, and gave him his meals in an earthenware basin. As he sat in his corner all by himself, the old man would often look sorrowfully at the table with tears in his eyes but he did not complain.

— — — — — — — — — — — — — — — — — — — —

One day, while the old man was thinking sadly of the past, the earthenware basin, which he could scarcely hold in his trembling hands, fell to the ground and was broken. The young wife scolded him for being so careless, but he did not reply; he only sighed deeply. Then she bought him a wooden bowl at the market for a penny and gave him his meals in it.

— — — — — — — — — — — — — — — — — — — —

Some days afterward, his son and daughter saw their little four-year-old son sitting on the ground trying to fasten together some pieces of wood.

— —

"What are you making my boy?" asked his father.

— —

_____

*Adapted from _Grimm's Complete Fairy Tales_, n.d.

"I am making a little bowl for papa and mamma to eat their food in when I grow up," he replied.

— — — — — — — — — — — — — — — — — — — —

The husband and wife looked at each other without speaking for some time. At last they began to cry, and went and brought their old father back to the table. From that day on, the old man always took his meals with them and was never again treated unkindly.

◀▶ ◀▶ ◀▶ ◀▶ ◀▶ ◀▶ ◀▶ ◀▶ ◀▶ ◀▶ ◀▶ ◀▶ ◀▶ ◀▶ ◀▶ ◀▶ ◀▶ ◀▶ ◀▶

STORY MAPPING — BEFORE THE TELLING

To further illustrate the effect that internalized structure has on one's ability to comprehend (or tell) a story, consider a story map drawn before a storytelling. Such an exercise will call into conscious memory the story structures operating subconsciously and clearly define the nature of the slotting process.

To "See" Story Structure in Its Generic Form

Tell the students (audience) that they are about to hear a story. Ask them what they think they might hear, or what, generally, they think is going to happen. Once they are over shrugging and looking about, they often indicate such things as beginnings, middles, ends, problems, characters, resolutions, and conclusions, perhaps morals. They list most, if not all, of the generic slots that define story as story. Then ask them to put the items in their list in the order in which they think they will hear them in the story. The students will have mapped "story" as they know it. They cannot slot story content, as yet, because they have none with which to work.

To Impose a Model for Slotted Content upon the Story (Constructing)

Tell the students (audience) only the following storied information.

"The Two Old Women's Bet"*

◄►◄►◄►◄►◄►◄►◄►◄►◄►◄►◄►◄►◄►◄►◄►◄►◄►◄►◄►

One time, there was two old women got to talkin' 'bout the menfolk. 'Bout how foolish they could act, and what was the craziest durn'd fool thing their husbands had ever done. Got to arguin', then, which of their husbands was the sillier. Made a bet, finally, which one o' them could make the bigger fool outa her old man. [Stop.]

◄►◄►◄►◄►◄►◄►◄►◄►◄►◄►◄►◄►◄►◄►◄►◄►◄►◄►◄►

The students already "know" story. They will already have imposed their mental models for story upon the whole, even though they have heard only a fraction of it. And, contrary to mechanistic views which suggest that the listeners don't know content until they have heard it, the students will also slot the entire story. They will then listen to the remainder of the telling with a set of presuppositions in place. The story itself will confirm or contradict these predictions; each listener will make necessary adjustments and will reposition accordingly. To show students that they have, indeed, constructed the entire story, content and structure, in concert with mental models that they already possess, let each student map the story—before hearing the rest of it. A web is best for this exercise. The webbing in figure 2.2 was made by an adult.

Then finish telling the story. The students will readjust their internal story maps as their presuppositions interact with the story. After the telling, two additional exercises can be used to illustrate the process of repropositioning that takes place when the mental model imposed upon the external material (the story) is contradicted by the story itself.

1. Ask the students to remember their original predictions. Have each student identify the point in the story at which his or her predictions were not confirmed by what was happening in the story. What had each student predicted? What happened in the story instead? At that moment, what changes or additional predictions did each student make about the story?

2. Using the webbing device, remap the story. Compare the pre-telling construction with the web derived from the story itself. Where, when, and why did the pre-telling map diverge from the post-telling map?

Try this exercise using printed material for examination of a story both before and after reading.

---

*Adapted from Chase 1951.

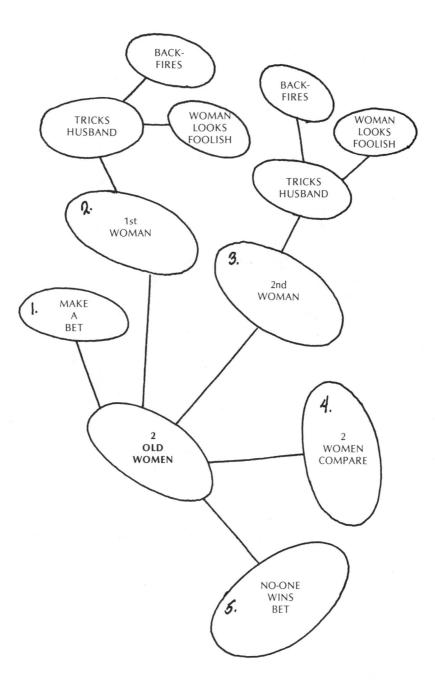

Fig. 2.2. An adult's webbing.

TAILORING A STORY—STRUCTURE

Storytellers understand that stories in their repertoires are not recited word-for-word with each retelling. Because a teller holds a story in memory in the form of a story structure plus related content, the told story is a result of a process of "slotting" content into structure. While the story is essentially the same story with each retelling, some linguistic and paralinguistic (interpretive) elements may change from one telling to the next. Some differences are the expected result of the natural process of rebuilding the story. However, some are the deliberate effects of the storyteller experimenting with elements of delivery, or accommodating the story to a given level of audience capability and expectation.

A storyteller might consider learning to tell the same story using two different structural arrangements, a deliberate tailoring to create two versions of a given story. Developing the capability to tell the same material in two different patterns has some advantages in terms of the teller's flexibility in accommodating audiences.

Since a story structure is a way of organizing information, a story's content can be arranged—"storied"/told—using more than one structural device. The device itself can be chosen, then, to meet the needs of the audience. For example, young audiences (second grade or younger) especially enjoy the repetitious language play afforded by cumulative pattern stories which wind and unwind lists, names, and noises. Such language patterns make a story highly predictable, are easy to remember, and reinforce language and literary development. Winding and unwinding is a good memory game.

To tailor a story in order to be able to tell it using a second structural arrangement, the teller must recognize the pattern of the story as he or she first found and learned it. For instance, *Who's in Rabbit's House?* (Aardema 1977) is given as a substitution story, in which one animal after another confronts "the long one," the bad animal that has taken control of Rabbit's house. Each animal tries to remove the bad animal from the house, with no success. Aardema provides a sequence that is replete with noise, character posturing and movement, and talk. The story, as given, allows for audience chanting of the standard reply of the bad animal, but the wonderful noise words which accompany each event are never repeated. Younger children would enjoy making the noises, but cannot, since each occurs only once. However, the same story content, recast as a winding and unwinding cumulative pattern, will allow maximum audience participation by increasing content predictability. (The cumulative pattern will also lengthen the story.)

As published, the story structure looks like this:

Setting: Events in setting category

1. Rabbit returns home one evening to find house occupied by a bad animal.

2. When she demands entrance to her house, the animal replies, "I AM THE LONG ONE! I EAT TREES AND TRAMPLE ON ELEPHANTS! GO AWAY, OR I WILL TRAMPLE ON YOU!"

(Repetitious language to be chanted with each story event. Sing or say ominously. Gregorian chant effective.)

Problem—Rabbit cannot get into her house; the bad animal will not come out. She contemplates her situation, but can find no solution. She cries, "WALLOO, WALLOO, WALLOO."

Event sequence

(Each animal in sequence comes along the path, and tries to extricate the bad animal. For each, use repeat chant above.)

1. Frog. (Set up for resolution.) "NUH!" says Rabbit. "You are too small. SEMM!"

2. Jackal. Pushes sticks against house — "KABAK!" — to burn the bad animal out.

3. Leopard. Tries to scratch through the roof — "ZZT! ZZT! ZZT!"

4. Elephant. Attempts to trample house — "GUMM! GUMM! GUMM!"

5. Rhinoceros. Charges house with intent of tossing it into the lake — RAS! RAS! RAS!" Tosses rabbit into the lake instead.

Resolution — Frog pretends to be the spitting cobra — "SSIH! SSIH! SSIH!" Frightens the bad animal out of Rabbit's house.

Conclusion — The bad animal, a caterpillar, comes out of Rabbit's house, eyes looking everywhere — "RIM! RIM! RIM!" — legs jerking about — "VITYO! VITYO! VITYO!" All of the animals laugh. The smallest of them provided the solution after all.

To convert the story to a winding/unwinding pattern, attention must be given to the "Event sequence." Other structural elements may be used as described above. If the same content were reslotted into a cumulative device, the following kind of pattern is one of the possible products.

Event sequence — (Each event is preceded by a conversation between Rabbit and the animal trying to help her. Rabbit tells her trouble to each animal, motivating each to make an attempt to remove the bad animal; and after each attempt there is more trouble.)

1. Frog's attempt.

    Frog: Rabbit, why aren't you sitting in your doorway?

    Rabbit: I cannot. A bad animal is in my house. It will not come out, and I cannot get in.

    Rabbit rudely rejects Frog's offer to help, insisting that Frog is too small — SEMM! Frog hides behind a bush to watch.

2. Jackal's attempt.

    Jackal: Rabbit, ... (same as Frog, above).

    Cumulative sequence begins

    Rabbit: I cannot. A bad animal is in my house. It will not come out, and I cannot get in. Frog said she could help, but she is so small, so small, so small — SEMM! What can she do?

    Jackal: (Turning to Rabbit's house.) WHO'S IN RABBIT'S HOUSE?

    Bad Animal: I am ... (as in first structural outline).

Jackal is put off by the voice, tries to slink away, but Rabbit calls him back. Jackal collects many sticks, pushes them against the door of the house—"KABAK!"—and explains, amid Rabbit's protests, that he will burn the bad animal out. Rabbit chases Jackal away, begins to pick up the sticks—"KABEK! KABEK! KABEK!" Frog laughs softly to herself—"GDUNG, GDUNG, GDUNG."

3. Leopard's attempt.

> Leopard: (Seeing Rabbit collecting the sticks.) What are you doing, Rabbit? Are you putting sticks there to hide your house?

Cumulative sequence begins

> Rabbit: No, not that. A bad animal is in my house. It will not come out, and I cannot get in. Frog said she could help, but she is so small, so small, so small—SEMM! What can she do? Jackal wanted to burn him out, so he pushed this pile of sticks against the door—KABAK! Now I must remove them—KABEK! KABEK! KABEK!

> Leopard: (Turning to Rabbit's house.) WHO'S IN RABBIT'S HOUSE?

> Bad Animal: (As given.)

Leopard responds with a threat of his own; he jumps to the roof of Rabbit's house, and begins to shred it with his claws—"ZZT! ZZT! ZZT!" Rabbit protests that she does not need such help, and Leopard retreats. Rabbit climbs to the roof to make repairs—"BET, BET, BET." Frog laughs more loudly.

4. Elephant's attempt.

> Elephant: (Seeing Rabbit patting and smoothing the roof of her house.) What has happened, Rabbit? Does your roof leak?

Cumulative sequence begins

> Rabbit: No, not that. A bad animal is in my house. It will not come out, and I cannot get in. Frog said she could help, but she is so small, so small, so small—SEMM! What can she do? Jackal wanted to burn him out, so he pushed this pile of sticks against the door—KABAK! I had to remove them—KABEK! KABEK! KABEK! Leopard tried to tear my house to bits—ZZT! ZZT! ZZT!—and eat him. Now I must repair my roof—BET, BET, BET.

> Elephant: (Turning to Rabbit's house.) WHO'S IN RABBIT'S HOUSE?"

> Bad Animal: (As given.)

Elephant becomes quite incensed, since elephants customarily do the trampling. Elephant backs up, then runs at Rabbit's house, her feet making deep holes in Rabbit's yard. GUMM! GUMM! GUMM! Rabbit leaps in front of her, and manages to wave her off. Elephant walks on to the lake. Frog laughs still more loudly.

> Rabbit: Stop laughing, Frog. I can hear you! Rabbit takes her hoe, and begins to fill and smooth the holes left in the yard. KOK! KOK! KOK!

5. Rhinoceros's attempt.

> Rhinoceros: (Seeing Rabbit working in the yard with the hoe.) What are you doing, Rabbit? Are you making a farm here by your house?

Cumulative sequence begins

> Rabbit: No, not that. A bad animal is in my house. It will not come out, and I cannot get in. Frog said she could help, but she is so small, so small, so small—SEMM! What can she do? Jackal wanted to burn him out, so he pushed a pile of sticks up against the door—KABAK! I had to remove them—KABEK! KABEK! KABEK! Leopard tried to tear my house to bits—ZZT! ZZT! ZZT!—and eat him. I had to repair my roof—BET, BET, BET. Then Elephant wanted to trample him—GUMM! GUMM! GUMM!—but she almost trampled my house. She made these holes in my yard. Now I must fill them—KOK! KOK! KOK!

> Rhinoceros: (Turning to Rabbit's house.) WHO'S IN RABBIT'S HOUSE?

> Bad Animal: (As given.)

Rhinoceros, fuming, makes threatening comments and gestures, puts his head down, and charges at Rabbit's house, determined to toss both house and bad animal into the lake. Rabbit intervenes by leaping onto and clinging to Rhinoceros's horn. With his poor eyesight, Rhinoceros thinks he has hooked the house, throws his head back, and pitches Rabbit high into the air. WEO! WEO! WEO! DILAK! DILAK! DILAK! She lands in the lake.

Resolution—Repeat as in first structural outline.

Conclusion—An additional full cumulative round which includes the Rhinoceros action can be inserted into the conclusion. After Frog has dispatched the bad animal, all of the characters gather in front of Rabbit's house. She tells them the story from the beginning.

Cumulative sequence begins

Rabbit: A bad animal was in my house. It would not come out, and I could not get in. Frog said she could help, but she is so small, so small, so small—SEMM!. What could she do? Jackal wanted to burn him out, so he pushed a pile of sticks up against the door—KABAK! I had to remove them—KABEK! KABEK! KABEK! Leopard tried to tear my house to bits—ZZT! ZZT! ZZT!—and eat him. I had to repair my roof—BET, BET, BET. Elephant wanted to trample him—GUMM! GUMM! GUMM!—but she almost trampled my house. She made holes in my yard. I had to fill them—KOK! KOK! KOK! Then Rhinoceros charged my house—RAS! RAS! RAS! He tossed me into the lake—WEO! WEO! WEO!—GNISH!—DILAK! DILAK! DILAK! But Frog got the bad animal out of my house." (Repeat as in resolution.)

Refer to the Aardema version (1977) for additional noises and dialogue. Younger audiences will enjoy the predictable, repetitious construction, and will be able to tell and do the story with the teller to a great degree. With older audiences the first structural version of the story might be more popular. Also try a cumulative restructuring of "Soap Soap Soap" (Chase, 1948).

POINT OF VIEW

◀▶ ◀▶ ◀▶ ◀▶ ◀▶ ◀▶ ◀▶ ◀▶ ◀▶ ◀▶ ◀▶ ◀▶ ◀▶ ◀▶ ◀▶ ◀▶ ◀▶ ◀▶ ◀▶ ◀▶

Have four people each choose to be one of the following characters:

Little Red Riding Hood

The Wolf

The Grandmother

The Woodcutter

Divide the rest of a group of people into four groups. Have each of the story characters tell the story of Little Red Riding Hood to one of the groups from his or her character's point of view.

Discuss and compare the reactions of each group to the story. Were some tellings funny? mysterious? matter-of-fact? scary?

Variation: choose other stories and other characters to reinforce the concept of point of view.

◀▶ ◀▶ ◀▶ ◀▶ ◀▶ ◀▶ ◀▶ ◀▶ ◀▶ ◀▶ ◀▶ ◀▶ ◀▶ ◀▶ ◀▶ ◀▶ ◀▶ ◀▶ ◀▶ ◀▶

ADDING MUSIC TO A STORY

The epic oral literature and many tribal oral histories were sung, often to musical or percussive accompaniment. The meter or cadence, the musical structure which bound the words, the repetition of phrases and rhyme schemes, all highly conventional, certainly aided memory to a significant degree. Though folk stories may not have been sung entirely, portions of these may have contained singing and chanting parts for storyteller and audience. While the music and style of these songs and chants may be lost in transcribed versions of such stories, a large number of stories retain verse in printed form. Countless other stories may once have contained musical elements and interpretations, but these dimensions of the stories may simply have been lost in print.

Audiences expect, rightly, to enact their ownership of a story. They know, after all, that the oral literature belongs to them. Singing and/or chanting built into a given story extends the audience's opportunity for investment. And because many transcribed stories either lack musical notation or are devoid of verse, the storyteller is obliged to develop and insert (sometimes invent and replace) lost musical elements. Some stories may not accept such inventions without seeming forced or unnatural, and some stories belong to cultures with which the teller might lack the necessary familiarity. Nevertheless, many stories remain that can take musical development.

For instance, in "The Singing Geese" (Whitney and Bullock 1925, Cothran 1954), the verse remains, though the music—it probably existed, given the many references to singing in the story—is gone. One enterprising storyteller invented musical notation for the verse, creating a haunting and beautiful melody. The audience itself invented a descant and low harmony on the spot. The result was magical. When the story had been told, the audience wanted the song again—and again—and again, to work with, refine, and enjoy.

*"The Singing Geese"**

LA LEE LOO.
COME QUILLA, COME QUILLA.
BUNG, BUNG, BUNG, QUILLA BUNG.

Likewise, the story of "Coyote and Locust" (Emrich 1947) contains verse that could very well have been sung. (Locust is "singing" in the story. Coyote specifically asks for his "song." Reference is made to "music.") Since no musical notation is given, the storyteller can either invent or research it. This author, having access to some oral authorities who know the Old Man Coyote stories, decided to research it. No luck. The music—surely there had once been some—was lost from memory, at least given limited investigation. The second solution, invention, was still an option. The result, a whole audience song, follows. The melody is intended to be flute-like since the story itself refers to that instrument. The author assumes flute, Native American form.

---

*In Whitney and Bullock 1925; Cothran 1954.

*"Coyote and Locust"**

Locust. Locust.
Playing a flute. Playing a flute.
High up on the pine tree bough.
Sweetly singing.
Playing a flute. Playing a flute.

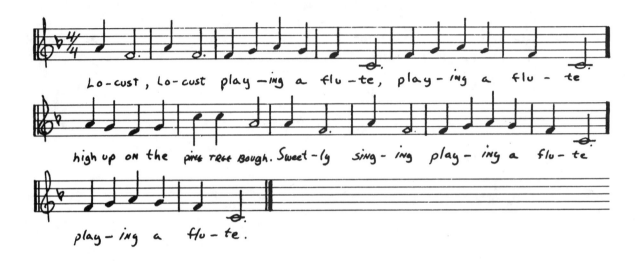

"One Trick Too Many" (Ginsburg 1973) does not specify verse or make deliberate reference to music, but invites it nevertheless. Fox, the main character (see "Travels of a Fox," Literature Committee 1950), plays a series of tricks in a substitution story, a familiar pattern. Each new trick begins with Fox begging to be allowed into a house or cabin for the night. Indeed, the success of his tricking depends upon the inhabitants of each abode opening the door for him, allowing him access to their home, and, subsequently, to their belongings. Since all of the story characters know fox to be a trickster, they are reluctant and suspicious. His end is achieved, in each case, by his dogged determination, which is made plain as he pleads his case at each door and convinces the other characters of his utter misery. Rather than using the storyteller alone to narrate Fox's mewlings, the audience can sing or chant a storyteller-invented verse in which Fox grovels and moans woefully.

*In Emrich 1947.

*"One Trick Too Many"**

[Preceding narrative:] Fox then walked onto the porch and directly to the door. He pounded upon the door with his paw. [Add sound.] A voice from within said, "Who's there?" [Change voice for each house/character.] "It is I, Fox!" said Fox. "Well, what do you want, then, Fox?" said the voice. "Oh…," said Fox. [Sound sincere, but with a hidden agenda somewhat evident.) "I really don't want much. I just need a place to spend the night. I won't take up much room." [Voice behind the door, with finality:] "Go away, Fox! We scarcely have room enough here for ourselves!" At that, Fox commenced to whining and begging and pleading…. [Assume convincing supplicant posture and sing verse:]

Oh please. Oh please. Oh please.
I don't want much, not much.
A scrap of floor,
Behind the door,
My weary head to touch, to touch.
My weary head to touch.

Oh please. Oh please. Oh please.
I beg you, hear my woes.
I ache in a way,
From walking all day.
And my head hurts in my toes, my toes.
My head hurts in my toes.

Oh please. Oh please. Oh please
Treat kindly my despair.
I'll stay in one place,
With my tail o'er my face.
And you'll never know that I'm there, I'm there.
And you'll never know that I'm there.

---

*Adapted from Ginsburg 1973.

Both verse and music are formula compositions, highly conventional, and easily remembered for repetition.

Finally, even stories that contain no chanting, music, or verse can accommodate these features if song is invented and inserted in a manner compatible with the nature of the story. The storyteller, however, must be careful not to violate story line and flow. The inserted effects must feel natural. "The Seventh Father of the House" (Asbjornsen and Moe 1960) is a very efficient cumulative story that has neither music nor verse in its published form. With each new event in the cumulative sequence, a traveller approaches a given father of a house and requests lodging. The traveller puts a simple question—"Good evening, Father. Can you put me up for the night?"—the request could also be set to verse and sung:

"The Seventh Father of the House"*

Good evening, Father.
The day is at end.
I am on a long journey,
And beg from you, friend,
Bed for sleep,
Bread for keep,
A song and a story will weariness mend.

---

*Adapted from Asbjornsen and Moe 1960.

Good ev-ening, Fa-ther the day is at end. I am on a jour-ney, and beg from you friend, bed for sleep, bread for keep, a song and a stor-y will wear-i-ness mend.

Finally, many winding and unwinding cumulative stories are easily chanted or sung without the need for verse invention. The voice falls so very easily into the chant pattern and certain rhythms like the childhood taunt, "NAH NAH NAH NAAAH NAH." Perhaps we simply "know" those seemingly natural intervals. Though this author also likes the effective spoken repetition in "Why Mosquitoes Buzz in People's Ears" (Aardema 1975), the unwinding, handled by King Lion as he unravels the mystery of Mother Owl's refusal to wake the sun, can also be sung.

"Why Mosquitoes Buzz in People's Ears"*

So, it was Mosquito who annoyed the Iguana, who frightened the Python, who startled the Rabbit, who alarmed the Crow, who warned the Monkey, who broke the branch which fell upon the Owlet. And now Mother Owl will not waken the Sun so that the day can come.

So it was Mosquito — (v1) who an-noyed the Ig-uana — who (v2) frightened the Python — who (v3) startled the Rabbit — And now Mother Owl — will not wa-ken the Sun so the day can come.

---

*In Aardema 1975.

For the storyteller who is looking for stories that include singing, a resource such as McDonald's motif index (McDonald 1982) can help. The key words "singing," "song," "music," "dance," "whistle," etc., appear in story titles and/or descriptions and suggest likely material. Try working with "The Do-All Ax" (Courlander 1957): "Bo Kee Meeny, Dah Ko Dee. Field need plantin', get off my knee." Consider adding notation to "The Tar Baby (Water Well Version)" (Botkin 1944): "Cha Ra Ra, will you, will you, can you? Cha Ra Ra, will you, will you, can you?" Find "Fox Sings a Song" (Jacobs 1916, 1967) or "The Fox Who Wanted to Whistle" (Barlow 1966). Try musical additions with these and other similarly patterned stories.

Singing, song, and verse seem to be a natural and integral part of storying, but are elements of practice that are often largely forgotten, lost because of the effects of story collection and transcription on the sounds of stories.

Storytellers who are able to reinvest even some of their material with song, chant, verse, and music will discover ready audiences, and will bring a relatively unpracticed dimension back to the oral literature.

MAKING A BALLAD

Ballads, stories in verse form, contain all of the elements of "story" that make stories recognizable. Ballads, however, constrain the telling (building) of the story to the specific requirements of the verse, such as rhyme scheme and meter. Ballads can serve as good raw materials for the making of stories: a ballad can be "retold" in prose (see Livo and Rietz 1986, 168-71). Conversely, ballads can also be constructed from stories, though this reverse process is more difficult, owing to the tighter restrictions of poetic form.

To make a ballad, the storyteller must first find a suitable story. A straightforward, efficient, uncomplicated problem encountered/problem solved story is best. Long, involved, complicated plots are difficult to convert to verse form unless one is prepared to create a miniature epic. Next, the teller must draw upon his or her familiarity with common folk tunes and the structure of sung verse. Even tellers who will not admit to singing (much) know such songs as "My Bonnie," or "On Top of Old Smokey," or "Clementine." The stuff of childhood goes into permanent memory early, and remains indelibly imprinted.

For a beginning exercise, combine the content of a given story with the structure of a well-known song. The idea is to tell the essense of the story, retaining all critical information, but to refine and simplify the content to fit it to the more limited and efficient form imposed by the verse. While the first try may be awkward and require trial attempts with several songs in order to get the right "fit," control of the process will develop. This exercise is also interesting because of the unusual circumstance of "slotting" a known content into a known, but very restricted, form.

"The Flying Shoes"*

◄►◄►◄►◄►◄►◄►◄►◄►◄►◄►◄►◄►◄►◄►◄►◄►◄►◄►◄►

(tune: "Comin' Through the Rye")

Long ago, an old, old man came walking to a town.
With magic shoes upon his feet, he did not touch the ground.
He rested 'neath a tall birch tree;
He meant to take a snooze.
A servant boy did happen by and stole away his shoes.

When the boy pulled on the shoes, they turned him upside down.
He floated over hill and dale and tumbled into town.
The young boy's master saw the shoes,
And put them on his feet.
Those magic shoes upended him and tossed him in the street.

The master was uplifted, for he landed in a tree.
He cried to people standing there, "Please take these shoes from me!"

The tax collector did oblige;
He put the shoes right on.
His money bags were shaken out, his tax collections gone.

The taxman's wife retrieved her man. The shoes he threw away.
They landed near the old, old man, as 'neath the tree he lay.
The old man laughed and took his shoes;
Their magic ways he knew.
And with his magic shoes returned, away toward home he flew.

◄►◄►◄►◄►◄►◄►◄►◄►◄►◄►◄►◄►◄►◄►◄►◄►◄►◄►◄►

For a second exercise, begin with a given story for content, but create the structure of the verse, setting it to original music. Gain some familiarity with the process using common songs as templates for ballad-making before taking this step.

---

*Adapted from Jameson 1973 by storytelling students at Eastern Montana College who constructed and sang the above ballad.

"Stone Soup"*

◀▶ ◀▶ ◀▶ ◀▶ ◀▶ ◀▶ ◀▶ ◀▶ ◀▶ ◀▶ ◀▶ ◀▶ ◀▶ ◀▶ ◀▶ ◀▶ ◀▶ ◀▶

Three soldiers came walking the road dressed in red.
Come rinkum, come tinkum, come tiddle um day.
Going home, they were tired and hungry, they said.
Come rinkum, come tinkum, kit ki me o linkum,
Come tiddle i iddle um day.

[Repeat italicized lines in remaining verses.]

They saw in the distance, a village ahead.
They hoped there to find a good meal and a bed.

But the villagers saw the three soldiers draw near,
And hid all their food, for they strangers did fear.

What's more, they were selfish and wished not to share.
They agreed, all, to claim that their larders were bare.

Such was the greeting at each door in town.
The answer was "no" when the soldiers went 'round.

But the soldiers were hungry clean down to their bones.
So they said to the people, "We'll make soup of stones."

As the villagers stood, their curiosity grew.
They gossiped about what the soldiers might do.

The soldiers did beg for the loan of a pot.
They stirred stones into water and boiled up the lot.

Stone soup with just water is really quite thin.
So the villagers "found" a few "things" to put in.

They brought out some carrots, a cabbage or two,
Salt, pepper, and barley, and beef for a stew.

They turned milk and potatoes right into the broth,
And fetched out the bread that was hid in the loft.

---

*Adapted from Brown 1947 by Sandra A. Rietz.

They lit up the torches and spread out the board,
And sat to a feast that was fit for a lord.

With the soup on the side, they ate roast and fresh bread.
Cider and wine found them all feeling fed.

They ate, and they drank far, far into the night,
And danced to the bagpipe beneath the moonlight.

Then, when the dancing did finally slow down,
The soldiers were led to the best beds in town.

Next morning a farewell was said in the street.
The people rejoiced such fine young men to meet.

For a soup from just stones is a magical thing;
Such wisdom that three simple soldiers should bring.

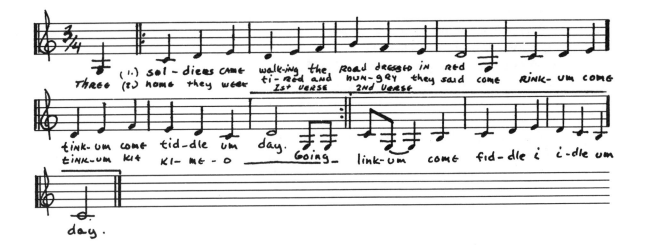

This effort, though an "original," is based upon years of experience with common folk song convention, and, in that it is a "formula" song complete with nonsense insertions, is a plagiarizing of the folk song tradition.

Ballad making only looks difficult. Slotting a story into the structure of a verse, especially if the verse is "known" (borrowed), is a game, much like the making of formula poetry. And using the restrictions of verse to "tell" a story clearly illustrates a basic principle of storytelling, the construction of a story by organizing content into form.

Mrs. Sara A. Price of Ottawa, Illinois, left this protest in her diary. The ballad, "The House-wife's Lament," is a story in song. That is essentially the definition of a ballad. Life was full of battles for this pioneer housewife of the plains, who lost sons in the Civil War.

The verses to this ballad can be sung to the familiar tune, "Cowboy's Lament." Another tune for this ballad is given in *The Folk Songs of North America* (Lomax 1960). A third possibility is to invent your own tune. That is the wonderful magic of ballads—they changed with each singer.

Try singing the ballad with several different tunes and enjoy the ballad. Appreciate the life that Sara Price lived. What is the same today? What is different?

"The Housewife's Lament"*

◄►

One day I was walking, I heard a complaining,
And saw an old woman the picture of gloom.
She gazed at the mud on her doorstep ('twas raining)
And this was her song as she wielded her broom.

Chorus:

Oh, life is a toil and love is a trouble,
Beauty will fade and riches will flee,
Pleasures they dwindle and prices they double,
And nothing is as I would wish it to be.

There's too much of worriment goes to a bonnet,
There's too much of ironing goes to a shirt,
There's nothing that pays for the time you waste on it,
There's nothing that lasts us but trouble and dirt.

[Repeat chorus.]

In March it is mud, it is slush in December,
The midsummer breezes are loaded with dust,
In fall the leaves litter, in muddy September
The wallpaper rots and the candlesticks rust.

[Repeat chorus.]

---

*Reprinted from Price 1956, 28 and Lomax 1960, 124, 133.

There are worms on the cherries and slugs on the roses,
And ants in the sugar and mice in the pies,
The rubbish of spiders no mortal supposes
And ravaging roaches and damaging flies.

[Repeat chorus.]

With grease and with grime from corner to center,
Forever at war and forever alert,
No rest for a day lest the enemy enter,
I spend my whole life in a struggle with dirt.

[Repeat chorus.]

◄►

Now that you are familiar with the ideas and feelings of the ballad, look at your own life. Each of us is a variety of people: wives, husbands, sons, daughters, parents, storytellers, students, teachers, librarians, recreation leaders, religious educators. How can we write laments that will describe our lives? What are the conditions in our lives that we could substitute for the conditions in this ballad?

Write your own lament and share it with others. The laments of many storytellers could be written, illustrated, and included in a book of laments for others to read and sing.

Variations: Rewrite "The Housewife's Lament" in a variety of other forms. For example, use modern setting, future setting, science fiction, poetry, interview form, reader's theater format, folk tale, newspaper article, or mystery. Essential to writing these variations is to describe the person who wrote the ballad, describe the setting, and identify the person's problem.

REFERENCES

Aardema, Verna. 1977. *Who's in Rabbit's House? A Masai Folktale.* New York: Dial.

_____. 1975. *Why Mosquitoes Buzz in People's Ears.* New York: Dial.

Asbjornsen, Peter Christian, and Jorgen Moe. 1960. *Norwegian Folk Tales.* New York: Viking.

Barlow, Genevieve. 1966. *Latin American Tales: From the Pampas to the Pyramids of Mexico.* Chicago: Rand McNally.

Botkin, B. A. 1944. *A Treasury of American Folklore*. New York: Crown.

Brown, Marcia. 1947. *Stone Soup: An Old Tale*. New York: Scribner.

Chase, Richard. 1948. *The Grandfather Tales*. Boston: Houghton Mifflin.

_____. 1951. *Wicked John and the Devil*. Boston: Houghton Mifflin.

Cothran, Jean. 1954. *With a Wig, With a Wag, and Other American Folktales*. New York: McKay.

Courlander, Harold. 1957. *Terrapin's Pot of Sense*. New York: Henry Holt.

Emrich, Marion Vallat. 1947. *The Child's Book of Folklore*. New York: Dial.

Ginsburg, Mirra. 1973. *One Trick Too Many—Fox Stories from Russia*. New York: Dial.

Grimm's Complete Fairy Tales. n.d. Garden City, N.Y.: Doubleday.

Harris, John. 1986. American Folktales. *The Atlantic* 257 (April): 32-33.

Hayes, Joe. 1982. *Coyote and....* Santa Fe, N.M.: Mariposa.

Jacobs, Joseph. 1916, 1967. *European Folk and Fairy Tales*. New York: Putnam.

Jameson, Cynthia. 1973. *The Flying Shoes*. New York: Parents Magazine Press.

The Literature Committee of the International Kindergarten Union. 1950. *Told under the Green Umbrella*. New York: Macmillan.

Lomax, Alan. 1960. *The Folk Songs of North America*. Garden City, N.Y.: Doubleday.

MacDonald, Margaret Read. 1982. *The Storyteller's Sourcebook: A Subject, Title and Motif Index to Folklore Collections for Children*. Detroit, Mich.: Neal-Schuman.

Price, Sara A. 1956. "The Housewife's Lament." In *Sing Out*. Volume 6. New York: People's Songs.

Whitney, Annie Weston, and Caroline Canfield Bullock. 1925. *Folklore from Maryland*. Volume XVIII. New York: Memoirs of the American Folklore Society.

3

Presenting the Story

INTRODUCTION

The overall focus of the material contained in this chapter is "readiness." Many dimensions of readiness attend storytelling: the mental and physical readiness of the storyteller, the readiness of the audience to enter into the story, the readiness of the story to be told (as the teller has developed it), and the readiness of the oral language capacities of both audience and teller. Getting ready, for both audience and storyteller, and the degree of story readiness are primary to successful storytelling.

The activities collected here address the several dimensions of readiness specified above. For the teller, the exercises presented include those intended to produce both physical and mental readiness, to aid aspects of story readiness dealing with body interpretation (visual imagery), and to extend linguistic capacities for telling. For the audience, suggestions focus upon ritual objects and protocols used by storytellers to bring the audience into the story—to conduct the "crossing over" into the time and place of the story.

Most, if not all, activities in storytelling that build some dimension of readiness for the telling of the story hold in common the element of concentration. While this particular selection of exercises describes some variety of actual activity, all exercises are intended to provide the story-teller with a means to achieving the intensity of focus of mental and physical energy needed to be a good storyteller.

HOW TO ENTER THE STORY

Ritual Openings and Closings

◀▶ ◀▶ ◀▶ ◀▶ ◀▶ ◀▶ ◀▶ ◀▶ ◀▶ ◀▶ ◀▶ ◀▶ ◀▶ ◀▶ ◀▶ ◀▶ ◀▶ ◀▶

"A story, a story
Let it come.
Let it go."

(West African)

"We do not really mean ...
We do not really mean ...
That what we say is true."

(Ashanti ritual opening)

Ritual openings are similar to the theater houselights dimming and the curtains being drawn. They prepare the audience for the story to come. "Once upon a time" is an automatic signal for listeners.

Study ritual openings and closings from throughout the world. For sources, see *Storytelling: Process and Practice* (Livo and Rietz 1986, 187-94).

Now, create your own ritual opening and closing. Share these inventions with others.

◀▶ ◀▶ ◀▶ ◀▶ ◀▶ ◀▶ ◀▶ ◀▶ ◀▶ ◀▶ ◀▶ ◀▶ ◀▶ ◀▶ ◀▶ ◀▶ ◀▶ ◀▶

Story-Initiating Quotations

Though stories often teach lessons, many do not restate their lessons as a proverb or moral at the end of the tale. In some storytelling traditions, adding a moral gives insult to the intelligence of the audience. But the old sayings are like bullets—clear, clean, unadorned observations on the nature of human behavior and the human condition. And many of them are funny: We experience our most serious and introspective moments when we are able to laugh at ourselves.

"Sayings" in the context of a storytelling program, not as morals which put meanings on stories, but as story beginnings work very well. Somehow these proverbs, used before the stories, retain their own identities as special forms of folklore. They seem more direct and precise before the story; they retain their own special integrities. And, rather than telling, after the fact, what an audience should have concluded from a particular story, the initiating proverb acts to stimulate predicting.

All cultures have a rich collection of proverbial sayings. Even Murphy's Laws and other similar "rules" are cast in proverbial form, i.e., "Blessed is he who expects nothing, for he shall not be disappointed" (Dickson 1978). These little "bits" can provide fine openings for individual stories.

- For "The Coyote and the Locust" (Hayes 1982):

  "My friend, It's not the learning that's important, but the leaning. You must lean toward your questions, your problems; lean slowly, so that you don't bend the solution too badly out of shape." (Peter Blue Cloud)

- For "Happy-Go-Lucky" (Wiesner 1972):

  "For every rip, there is a patch." ("For every man, there is a woman. No falta un roto para un descosido.") (Aranda 1977)

- For "The Day It Snowed Tortillas" (Hayes 1982):

  "He who has little to lose has little to worry about." ("El que poco tiene, poco teme.") (Aranda 1977)

- For "Stone Soup" (Brown 1947):

  "Whoever says 'A' must also say 'B'." ("Wer sagt 'A' muss auch 'B' sagen.") (Family saying)

- For "Jack and the Three Sillies" (Chase 1950)

  "A fair exchange is no robbery." (Brunvand 1978)

Proverbs can be chosen to suit the theme or lesson of the story or to fit the story subject. The following bits might be used with frog stories:

"A frog would leap from a throne of gold into a puddle."

"Oh, to be a frog, my lads, and live aloof from care."

"The frog's own croak betrays him."

"A frog in the well knows not of the ocean." ("Ido no Kawazu taikai wo shirazu.") (Japanese proverb)

"The frog flew into a passion, and the pond knew nothing about it." ("Gomame no hagi-shiri.") (Japanese proberb)

(Donaldson 1980)

Other proverbs can be found in a variety of sources: *The Farmer's Almanac*, the works of James Fennimore Cooper, the writing of Emerson, Sandburg, and Benjamin Franklin (*Poor Richard's Almanac* and *The Way to Wealth*). Listen to conversations; begin collecting from relatives and friends. Especially find those proverbs which originated in your own native culture.

And what would you do with this Russian proverb? "When you live with a goat, you must get used to the bad smell" (Brunvand 1978). This one? "The YOO HOO you YOO HOO into the forest is the YOO HOO you get back" (Dickson 1978). Or this one? "You can't tell how deep a puddle is until you step into it" (Dickson, 1978).

Monitoring Pre-telling Protocols

When the storyteller begins the storytelling, often with a ritual opening sequence (Livo and Rietz 1986), he or she brings the audience "over" into story time—the time in which the story takes place. This time cannot be reached by ordinary means, since it is a mystical and not a real (past/present/future) time. The audience participates in the story, in part, by "crossing over" into this realm of mystical cultural consciousness, in which more universal rules operate.

The storyteller takes the part of the ancient repository of the literature (the cultural cosmology), assuming the role of the old or ancient one, the "other." In this capacity, the storyteller gives body, language, habits, and talent to the story, but leaves his or her own daily personality behind. The teller therefore also must cross over into the realm of the stories.

While the storyteller conducts the ritual crossing for the audience, thus facilitating audience transition into story "time," no one can take the storyteller across. Yet the fact that the teller operates the ritual for the audience suggests that the teller makes the journey before the audience does, before the telling begins. By the time the teller comes to the audience, he or she has completed the crossing and presents himself or herself as the "other."

Since the teller must take himself or herself "over," the problem—a catch 22—becomes apparent. How do you get to a mystical place that must be reached by extraordinary means when you have to act as your own medium? Many cultures solved this problem by constructing (through evolution) ritual protocols or routines for the storyteller, in order to instill in the teller the proper frame of mind and to invest the teller with his or her role. Some of these routines were conducted by priests; others were conducted by tellers themselves. Thus the storyteller was made ready to conduct a ritual crossing for an audience, and to call an audience over into a mystical time/place where he or she awaited them.

Although the ritual crossing into story time may no longer be a religious event, a teller still must become ready to tell. Readiness is a mental state in which the personality relinquishes control to the role of "storyteller," and in which the requirements of the story are allowed to manipulate and control the body without interference from one's collection of daily demands or concerns about petty embarrassments. At the least, the teller needs to make a last minute check on the memory routines that will run during story construction, thinking, at the same time, of the nature of the audience. There must be that final moment for the mental and physical deep breath before starting.

Many storytellers, like performers, run routines or protocols before a storytelling. A routine is primarily a mental exercise, probably the happy evolution of practice, which concentrates the mental and physical energy of the teller on the telling. The protocol helps to settle the teller: to bring the stories to be told into focus, to help the teller to control jitters, and to help the teller to assume the role of the "other," the ancient one who tells the stories. The routine readies the teller for the telling. In a sense, the teller "crosses over," at least to that frame of mental control that will permit the story to do its work.

1. CONSIDERING POSSIBILITIES—The storyteller must attend to the following: making the body ready, settling the mind, relegating the "self" to the role of observer, thinking about the requirements of audience and setting, checking story memories, and regulating the adrenalin.

Breathe slowly and deeply.

Do selected stretching exercises.

Try body extending movements, concentrating upon the body alone.

Walk.

Make a visual image of audience and setting; put yourself in that setting in your mind.

Focus attention on the stories or specific parts of the stories.

Tell selected pieces of several stories.

Concentrate on getting "inside" the storytelling and the stories to be told. ("Getting inside" is a mind exercise, a mental discipline.)

BE ALONE.

2. SELF-MONITORING—Many tellers have routines, but may not recognize the purposes that these serve, or that they even exist. Your awareness of personal readiness rituals and requirements can help to refine and focus the readying process as well as to help you to avoid tense moments or uncomfortable encounters with people and demands immediately before a storytelling.

Remember the last pre-telling routine. What did you do?

Which actions precede successful storytellings?

Which actions (or lack of actions) precede difficult storytellings?

Do any patterns become apparent?

Do some protocol items help, others hinder?

What are your pre-telling requirements?

How can these best be served?

Though many of us can tell a story with no apparent preparation—the "drop-of-the-hat" telling—we generally need some moments for readiness, however fleeting. This author has been confronted on numerous occasions with the offhand request to provide a story. Not having expected the asking, I freeze. (Contrary to what my friends or students might think, I do not walk about in a constant state of readiness to tell a story. I am me, most of the time, not the "other." And I cannot always, nor do I always want to perform the auto-hypnosis that is required for telling.) Even when I am able to come up with something, I must do a quick mental exercise which involves pulling away from myself and the immediate circumstance, taking a deep breath in the the mind and running some story memories. Sometimes I cannot pump up enough energy to conduct the mental rehearsal.

3.   FINDING ROUTINES—For the teller who has no, few, or ineffective pre-telling protocols, a deliberate effort to try one or more of the above mentioned exercises may help. A
storyteller who is ready tells a better story, exerts better control, handles the audience
with greater sensitivity, and commands a power in the telling situation. The ready teller
can enjoy a storytelling along with the audience.

Ritual Objects

◀▶ ◀▶ ◀▶ ◀▶ ◀▶ ◀▶ ◀▶ ◀▶ ◀▶ ◀▶ ◀▶ ◀▶ ◀▶ ◀▶ ◀▶ ◀▶ ◀▶ ◀▶

A teller can adopt a ritual object to hold stories, to identify stories, or to
act as a storytelling talisman of good luck. These objects include hats, all
kinds of wearing apparel, necklaces, sticks, aprons, bags, baskets, ropes, or
imaginary objects that "see" stories, "hold" stories, or "indicate" stories.

Richard Chase uses a walking stick and a bag. Jackie Torrence wears an
unusual medallion. Spencer Shaw lights a candle before storytelling and
blows it out at the end. Greg Denman uses a stool and a hat. John Stansfield
carries a woven knapsack. Opalanga Pugh shakes her gourd rattle. And
Sandie Rietz wears a special vest.

As you develop your storytelling talents, add a ritual object to your
personal storytelling habit. It may take experience with several ideas before
you find the "right" object for you.

◀▶ ◀▶ ◀▶ ◀▶ ◀▶ ◀▶ ◀▶ ◀▶ ◀▶ ◀▶ ◀▶ ◀▶ ◀▶ ◀▶ ◀▶ ◀▶ ◀▶ ◀▶

HOW TO DELIVER THE STORY

Teachers of storytelling must initiate people into a form of public speaking that contains
many of the aspects of control that also appear in performance. (A storyteller does not perform in
the theatrical sense, but this distinction has more to do with the intimacy of the audience-teller
relationship and the cultural role of the teller than with what a teller actually does during story
delivery.) Beginners, especially, can become overloaded when trying to remember how to handle
linguistic and paralinguistic effects along with the structure and content of the story.

Rather than allowing beginners to try to decide for themselves which elements of delivery
they will pay attention to and in what order, establish a formal protocol for systematic introduc-
tion of delivery technique. This formal protocol can bring better concentration and result in more
effective control.

Group Story Development

Story interpretation—adding lingustic and paralinguistic elements to a story—is difficult for tellers who have had little experience with storytelling. Even beginners, however, can provide one another with insight into how to encode a written version of a story into oral language. Try two group exercises designed to help inexperienced tellers "play" with the elements of delivery and with translation of written material into oral form.

1. Divide the larger group into five smaller groups. Assign each group the task of developing a different element for story delivery for the same story.

    Group 1—characterization through voice

    Group 2—characterization through posturing

    Group 3—visual imagery through body movement

    Group 4—interpretation through pitch and phrasing

    Group 5—audience participation through various means

    When each group has completed its task, reassign group memberships so that one member of the original five groups is now in the five new groups. Each of the new groups will thus have access to all of the techniques invented by the first five groups. Each group member presents the decisions about elements of delivery as discussed in the first grouping. One member of each second group, finally, is chosen to integrate all of the interpretive information into a full storytelling. Allow a week for these individuals to "work out" their respective deliveries; then have them present all five versions of the same story to the entire class.

2. Divide the larger group into several smaller groups. Give each group two stories, one that is the same and another that is different from those given to the other groups. Each group will read the stories. (Multiple copies that can be read out of class will save time.) Each group must develop a form of direct audience participation for each of the two stories, and then devise a means of teaching the audience its part or bringing the audience "in." Each group then chooses two individuals to tell the two stories for the entire group, using the participation inventions.

Such group activity serves at least two purposes. It allows novice tellers to solve encoding problems collectively, to create, invent, and design interpretive elements as a community. And it brings the nature and process of solving encoding problems to the conscious attention of the tellers.

Controlling the Elements of
Delivery—Practice

All beginning storytellers must learn to tell by telling. There is no other way. But, to make the first tellings more manageable, familiar structures (not necessarily familiar stories) should be chosen. The first exercise, then, aside from hearing and seeing storytellers work, is to learn to recognize structure, to learn to remember it, and to practice "slotting" ("telling" the story content inside the structure). When the first stories have been found and are being readied (memory), beginners can turn their attentions to elements of delivery.

This author introduces elements of delivery in a sequence, and asks tellers to concentrate on those aspects of story delivery that are assigned.

1. FOR THE VERY FIRST TELLING—Have each storyteller practice controlling for tense, for linguistic "garbage" (mazes and false starts), for interpretation of characters through voice, for pitch, and for phrasing—essentially all linguistic elements. The teller may sit or stand for story delivery. There is little concern at this point with what the body does; for example, the hands are free to do or not do what they will. This first story may be delivered while sitting.

2. FOR THE SECOND TELLING—Have each storyteller pay attention to the body, to facial expression, and to posturing, movement, and extension. While the attitude of the body should be natural throughout the telling, the teller is now becoming aware of the potential of the body for delivering visual imagery. The teller learns, here, to control for paralinguistic devices, while still incorporating all of the elements which applied to the first telling. This second story must be told while standing.

3. FOR THE THIRD TELLING—Have each storyteller develop audience interaction for a chosen story. Then have the teller devise a way of introducing the interaction to the audience or otherwise drawing the audience into the play. The teller must also retain, where appropriate, all of the linguistic and paralinguistic elements which applied to the first two tellings.

4. FOR THE FOURTH TELLING—Have each storyteller develop a prop for the telling of a story. Add the prop to all the techniques utilized for the first three tellings (audience interaction optional). The prop must be an integral part of the telling, a part of the story. It must not "take over" the story, but its purpose must also be clear. Props are discussed further in Livo and Rietz (1986).

Between each of the above tellings, introduce the students to technique and allow for opportunity both to practice and to hear other storytellers. The four tellings are spaced at two-week intervals.

Creating Visual Imagery

Written stories narrate visual imagery. The oral story depends upon narration to carry visual imagery to some lesser extent. When transcribed, an oral story will lose the paralinguistic aspects of visual imagery, and the storyteller is left with the problem of reinventing these effects. Which effects—interpretations through movement—are "right" for a transcribed story must be determined by the teller, using his or her knowledge of what oral stories look like. The transcribed version of a story may also contain some narrative description that the oral story never had. The collector may have felt obliged to describe with language what the storyteller described through movement, posturing, and general body expression. While the modern teller, who develops materials from print, cannot know precisely which narrated effects were intended for physical interpretation, he or she can make some informed decisions about which images to "do."

Using the following story as an example, we can find cues in the text that will provide likely instances for paralinguistic interpretation.

"The Frog's Saddle Horse"*

◀▶ ◀▶ ◀▶ ◀▶ ◀▶ ◀▶ ◀▶ ◀▶ ◀▶ ◀▶ ◀▶ ◀▶ ◀▶ ◀▶ ◀▶ ◀▶ ◀▶ ◀▶

Once upon a time, the Elephant and the Frog went courting the same girl, and at last she promised to marry the Elephant. One day the Frog said to her, "That Elephant is nothing but my saddle horse."

When the Elephant came to call that night, the girl said to him, "You are nothing but the Frog's saddle horse." When he heard this, the Elephant went off at once and found the Frog and asked him, "Did you tell the girl that I am nothing but your saddle horse?"

"Oh, no, indeed," said the Frog. "I never told her that!"

Thereupon they both started back together to see the girl. On the way, the Frog said, "Grandpa Elephant, I am too tired to walk any further. Let me climb up on your back."

"Certainly," said the Elephant. "Climb up, my grandson." So the Frog climbed up on the Elephant's back. Presently, he said, "Grandpa Elephant, I am afraid that I am going to fall off. Let me take some little cords and fasten them to your tusks to hold on by."

"Certainly, my Grandson," said the Elephant, and he stood still while the Frog did as he had asked. Presently, the Frog spoke again, "Grandpa Elephant, please stop and let me pick a green branch so that I can keep the flies off of you."

---

*In Donaldson 1980.

"Certainly, my Grandson," said the Elephant, and he stood quite still while the Frog broke off the branch. Pretty soon they drew near to the house where the girl lived. When she saw them coming, the Elephant plodding patiently along with the little Frog perched on his broad back, holding the cords in one hand and waving the green branch, she came to meet them, calling, "Mr. Elephant, you certainly are nothing but the Frog's saddle horse."

◄►

1. Find all of the verbs that suggest good and workable visual imagery.

> WENT (went off at once) suggests energy and emphasis—Elephant is at least put out.

> CLIMBED ("the Frog *climbed* up on the Elephant's back") suggests hand and arm TO MARK UP and HEIGHT, if not a minimal indication of climbing, perhaps rolling the hand as the arm rises.

> DID ("while Frog *did* as he asked") requires more specificity. Narration could be changed to "while Frog tied the cords in place." The change would allow knotting and tying motions. Or the same motions could supply the visual imagery for the narration as given.

> BROKE ("Frog broke off the branch") calls for a quick snapping motion, one- or two-handed.

> PLODDING ("plodding patiently") assumes an attitude, perhaps with head and shoulder or slight torso movement.

> PERCHED ("Frog perched upon his broad back") assumes an attitude—to make the body look "perched."

> HOLDING ("holding the cords") allows direct interpretation.

> WAVING ("waving the branch") allows direct interpretation. None of these movements needs to be elaborate. The story itself is very simple and efficient. The movements should be done in that style, but with deliberation and clarity.

2. Find cues to a character's facial expression and/or posture or movement in the character's speech.

> THAT ELEPHANT IS NOTHING BUT MY SADDLE HORSE. (pridefully, with a touch of scorn, pulling up to full height, perhaps with head set slightly to one side or thrown slightly back)

YOU ARE NOTHING BUT THE FROG'S SADDLE HORSE! (disgusted, feeling cheated, or betrayed and somewhat angry—perhaps with hands on hips, eyes slightly narrowed, head and torso forward—words articulated individually, sharply)

DID YOU TELL THE GIRL THAT I AM NOTHING BUT YOUR SADDLE HORSE? (dismayed, somewhat angered, demanding, leaning forward invasively—perhaps wagging the head with the words in a crisp manner)

OH, NO, INDEED! I NEVER TOLD HER THAT! (protesting innocently, wide-eyed and with honest surprise, as if to say, "Where did you hear that?"—beginning the line with a withdrawing of chin, head, then torso—literally taken aback)

Locate other quotations in the story. Work out attitude, facial expression, and character movement for each one. Good results can be obtained by climbing into the story—a mental exercise—and assuming the reality of and immediate perceptions of each character in turn. Given the circumstances, how would each character speak?

3. Read the story once again. Find the bits of narrative description that contain good visual imagery. What would the attitude of the body be for each one of these: "found the frog," "asked him," "started back together," "presently he said," "he stood still," "drew near to the house," "she saw them coming." While none of these requires acting per se, the body may add to the overall visual imagery in some manner.

The exercises above seem like too much trouble because they impose so much conscious attention upon the whole and may result in fragmentation. Certainly, as separate activities, these exercises are disruptive of fluency. Saying the language in the story as it would be said by people in this story's given circumstances, making the elements of narration and voice sound "right," might also bring the body into play. Too much attention to the effects of body attitude, posture, and movement could result in a delivery that appears unnatural and forced. However, a beginner's awareness of how stories cue the storyteller for the creation of visual imagery through movement can improve upon the "fencepost" style of story delivery.

Learning Movement

Stretching

Beginning storytellers are often still, tense and afraid of their own bodies. Though storytelling can be as natural as making conversation, the fact that one is "telling a story" sometimes strikes a terror that translates into rigor mortis. Asking a beginner to relax is a rather naive directive. (Likewise, telling the beginner to have fun.) One cannot "tell" a frightened or uncomfortable teller to let loose of the fencepost attitude during delivery. But a beginner can be "worked out" of that reluctance to free the body and to let the story in.

Use the following series of stretching postures with storytellers to encourage ease and freedom of movement; also use the exercises to help tellers to relax and to identify and release tense muscles.

1. Lie flat on the floor on your back. Beginning with the toes, tighten muscles in each separate body part, one part at a time. Hold the muscle taut, then release it. Will it to relax completely, and feel it let go. Once a given muscle is relaxed, go to the next. Do not again tense muscles that have been relaxed. Visualize each muscle separately during this exercise, and talk to it. Feel IT apart from the rest of the body.

   When all muscles are fully relaxed, imagine the body being so heavy and limp that it is sinking into the floor. Then imagine that the body is so light that it is floating free of gravity several feet off the ground.

This exercise is often most effective if "led," with one individual calling out one muscle/body part at a time, giving the command to tense, then release. A guided fantasy can help participants concentrate for sinking and floating. Concentration on the body is the key. Storytellers must learn to be sensitive to the body during storytelling, using those internal cues that the body provides to judge effectiveness of body use during telling. Most of us don't think much about what various parts of our bodies are doing when we perform a task; we tend to think about grocery lists and other things of similar significance. An exercise "leader" will help to keep a beginner's attention on the body and away from personal concerns.

2. With legs slightly spread, arms relaxed at sides, palms down, inhale slowly and lift arms straight out to shoulder level. Hold. Stretch arms out from the body, as if someone were pulling on them from both sides. Exhale. Turn palms face up. Inhaling slowly, again, continue lifting extended arms until hands almost touch overhead and the insides of the upper arms rest, but only lightly, against the ears. Stretch the entire body, beginning with the arms, as if someone were lifting the entire body from above by the fingers. Feel each subsequent body part stretch in its turn, from the fingers on down. Hold the posture, but exhale and relax. Inhale and stretch again. Release the position slowly while exhaling, returning to the initial posture by bringing the arms down in the same arc. Do not simply let go in a flop.

3. Assume the same standing position given in the second exercise. Follow the same steps, but raise only the right arm. Keep the left down and straight, but not tense. When the right arm is overhead, exhale while leaning over to the left, bent at the waist. Keep eyes forward; do not bend forward. Allow the left arm and hand to slide down the left leg. Imagine that the body is a series of articulating links, like beads on a wire. The bead string can be bent, but only so far. When the torso is bent to its maximum, inhale, then exhale. Return the right arm slowly to the overhead position while inhaling, then exhale to resume standing posture. Repeat for the left arm.

4. Assume the same standing posture given in the second exercise. Place the heels of the hands (fingers down, elbows bent) in the small of the back to either side of the backbone. While exhaling, allow the head to lead back and over. Head leading, bend as far backward as is possible. The hips will come forward. Inhale to return slowly to

standing position. (As one becomes more adept, greater stretching can be achieved by raising the hands from the small of the back to the rib cage and from that location to just under the shoulder blades.)

From a standing position, exhale slowly while allowing the body to bend forward as far as is possible. Relax the arms and torso completely—rag doll style. Place palms flat on the floor, if possible, but only if this can be done without tensing and stretching. Inhale to return slowly to standing.

For all exercises, concentrate on the body. Become aware of the location and action of each body part and work to develop a conscious knowledge of the internal signals sent "back" by each part. Work to achieve a sense of the place of the body in space and the relationship of one part of the body to another. Pay attention, especially, to extension—how far the body can reach into the space around it. Make an effort to clarify each movement in a stretch sequence.

Other stretching exercises can be found in exercise manuals. By far the most concise and easy to follow directions are given in *Hatha Yoga: Manual 1* (Samskirti and Veda 1977).

Games and Dances

One method for freeing novice storytellers from the stiffness that sometimes comes along with self-consciousness ("I'm going to tell a story! I can't move!") is the application of singing games, games, and singing dances for the purpose of learning to move, stand, and posture. Many old (children's) games make a play of just such body attitudes. Within the frame of reference of the play, and in the safety of the group, beginners can relax and feel their bodies move.

Freeze Posture Games

"Old Roger" (positioning and facial expression)

"Chē Weh" (positioning)

"Sally Go 'round the Sun" (interpretation through positioning)

"I Want to Be a Farmer" (interpretation through positioning)

Moving Posture Games

"Up on the Mountain" ("Two by Two") (interpretation/visual imagery)

"Go In and Out the Window" (visual imagery)

"Oats, Peas, Beans" (creative dramatics)

"Willobee" (invented motion)

"We're Marching 'round the Valley" (visual imagery)

Most of these and other common singing games and dances can be found in children's songbooks. A more complete reference is provided in *Storytelling: Process and Practice* (Livo and Rietz 1986, 330-88).

Postured Telling

Storytellers must become accustomed to executing movement, posturing, and talking simultaneously. Beginners, given the memory exercise involved in simply remembering and building the story, not to mention the fact of a live audience, are often taxed enough without having to remember such paralinguistic effects as movement. Exercises that combine telling with movement and posturing can help the teller to feel and know the body while making the language of the story.

Simple Postures

Begin telling a familiar story in standing posture. Break narrative, inhale, and assume shoulder stretch posture. Continue telling the story in this position. Break narrative, inhale, and assume arms overhead stretch posture. Resume telling. Exhale, reassume shoulder posture, resume telling. Exhale, return to standing posture and finish the story. Repeat this exercise, but with arms lifted out and forward as if sleepwalking. Try both palms down and palms up. Lift arms from front position to overhead and reverse the operation, pausing at each position to tell.

Tell a part of a story in "rag doll" position.

Tell part of a story with head down, neck bent forward, with head to left, with head to right, with head back, eyes on the ceiling.

Raise the right arm to shoulder stretch position, palm out. Turn the head; look at the back of the hand. Tell part of the story. Repeat for the left arm and hand.

Discover other postures which are not also so strenuous that they prevent talking, and tell in these positions. Work in both sitting and standing poses. Think about the body, its attitudes, and the internal signals that it sends back to the mind WHILE telling.

Descriptive Postures

Invent and assume a series of postures which also describe a thing, circumstance, or condition. Try the body in several of these positions, feeling physical extension and attitude. Imagine and develop a posture for:

A crow perched on a pole

A hanging plant with trailing vines

A starting official for a race, gun in hand

A timing official, same race, watch in hand

A nearsighted scribe working over a manuscript

A logger holding a running chain saw

A pole-vaulter holding a pole

A baker rolling dough

A gnarled, twisted tree

A child reaching for an object overhead.

Take one of these positions, using full extension. Concentrate on the manner in which the body is creating the image. Make adjustments. Feel the posture. See the image. Then, while holding the position, describe the image. Begin with "I am...," or "This is...." Supply enough descriptive detail to be able to use the verbal image as a standard from which to evaluate and further refine the posture itself.

Sculpture

Often, the storyteller can see appropriate posturing and invent body attitudes more easily for someone else than for himself or herself. The following exercise permits the teller to "sculpt" a posture using another individual as a model. Such activity allows a teller to invent, see, and play with a physical effect before trying it.

1. Each pair of storytellers selects a posture with which to experiment. The list provided in the previous exercise might be used to start.

2. One member of the pair serves as the manipulatable material, while the other pushes, bends, and twists the first into the proper position. Arms, legs, hands, feet, head, torso, even the face may be positioned and repositioned until the "right" attitude is achieved.

3. The "statue" (sculptee) holds the position—within reason.

4. Both members of the pair study and learn the posture. The statue, of course, learns the position by thinking about and collecting signals from the body—from the inside. The "sculptor" learns it visually, from the outside. Extension and attitude are thus examined from both perspectives.

5. The pair trade places. The sculptor assumes the posture that he or she thinks was created. The original statue, using his or her knowledge of the position gained from internal signals, checks and repositions the new statue.

Attention is given to extension, clarity of image, and information transmitted from the body itself. Memory, rehearsal for posturing, concentration, and confirmation of imagery are included in the exercise.

Moving Postures

Depending upon the demands of the story, the teller will be obliged to tell a story while holding a posture (see previous exercise) or while moving from one position to another. Several exercises can be used to develop a sophistication of body awareness and control during story construction.

1. Begin with the simple postures given in the discussion "Postured Telling." Tell not only at the "hold" positions, but also during movement. Keep movement slow, easy, and graceful. Deliberately try to tell a considerable amount of the story during this movement. Continue telling in the "hold" posture, then release slowly to the next position while talking.

2. Reexamine the story. Mark those parts of the narrative that suggest or even describe a posture. Tell the story, moving from one to the next of these postures in a sequence that matches the telling of the story. Hold each posture in turn. Work slowly, remembering the arm and torso extensions of previous exercises and maintaining as much of that extension as the postures themselves will allow, even if these feel unnatural. Monitor body signals and sensations throughout.

3. Try a series of sequenced movements that, themselves, describe a "story," for example, the germinating of a seed, the development of a thunderhead from a wisp of cloud, a kernel of popcorn — cold to popped, a flower wilting or closing up for the night. Again, work for full extension and clarity, and "listen" to the body as it feels itself in space.

4. Let single words or phrases suggest movement. Listen to a chosen word. Develop a visual image of the movement. Describe that image verbally if that will help. Work out the entire movement.

    TRY: stride, slouch, lounge, droop, stoop, totter, stumble, trip, crouch, grovel, cower, cringe.

    TRY: being very thin, having a pot belly, having one bad leg, walking with a cane, having uneven shoulders.

    TRY: riding a bus holding onto a ceiling strap, going out for a pass and making the perfect breadbasket catch, throwing a frisbie, catching a frisbie, walking a rail fence, splitting logs with an axe, washing clothes on a washboard, rinsing them and wringing them out.

Do these exercises standing. Go slowly. Work for the fullest extension and clarity that the attitude itself will allow. Collect body information.

5. Try moving posture done by a team. This exercise used with students and student story-tellers addresses dramatic movement, finding movement in stories and the idea of "story" itself. Arrange students in groups of five, at minimum. Have each group develop a "story" or scenario which requires movement. Their invention will have a clear beginning, middle, and end. Each member of the group will do a movement that is a part of the whole sequence. Each movement must derive from the movement that preceded it and initiate that which follows it. The final product will have each group member doing a separate movement which is a part of a whole.

The concept confuses people who have never tried this team operation before. Sometimes assigning tasks can help. One group will bake a cake—beginning, middle, and end. Another group will churn butter, starting with the cow. Yet another will make a set of dittoed worksheets, heaven forbid, beginning with the typewriter and the ditto master (original, if you add a thermofax), and finishing with the students who have to do it. The group must analyze the parts of each task, assign parts, work out the movements that belong to each, and then articulate the whole. Let people make noises for accompaniment, but disallow talking or narrative. The movement must carry the story. A superb round of movement was once constructed around the simple act of putting coins into a machine to get a can of pop. The group invented, reinvented, extended, expanded, got excited and added more, with the following result:

(Numbers indicate individuals as they appear.)

1, the pop machine, stands at ready, shaking, shivering, humming and "refrigerating." 2 digs deep into pocket, removes coins, sorts through same on palm of hand, finds wrong change (indicated by facial expression and long look at audience). 2 approaches three to make correct change. 3 digs through pocket. 2 and 3 manage to make change. 2 approaches machine and inserts coins. 1 begins to chink and rattle, then to "process." ("Process was an extraordinary bump and grind, with a "spit it out" action at end.) 1 spits out the can of pop. 2 misses it. The pop can hits the floor (2 conveys this with head and eyes, watching). 4, a baby, grabs can, shaking it with obvious delight. 5, mother, recovers can and returns it to 2. 2 opens can, which sprays pop in all directions. 2 looks into and upends can; it is empty. 2 begins to dig in pocket for change. Each player does his or her own action throughout: the machine refrigerates, the baby plays, the mother mothers, etc.

The best of these "task plays" are cyclic. The end reactivates the beginning, and all players can continue to do their movements while the play is going through its cycle.

As with movement exercises described previously, work for full extension and clarity of definition of movement. Work slowly and with deliberation. Concentrate and feel the body. Remember that the object of the play is to convey the task and its component parts to the audience through movement alone.

A very important part of every story is carried by the body, through physical interpretation. Such inventions either stand alone as carriers of information for the audience or further clarify and refine narrative description, monologue or dialogue. While we agree that storytelling is not performance in the theatrical sense, and that the storyteller is not "acting," the teller does need to be able to make his or her body work for the story to the extent that the story requires the development of visual imagery. Some degree of concentration, of body control, and of awareness can considerably enhance the telling of a story.

Jack Tales

◄►

Select one of the Jack tales from *The Jack Tales* by Richard Chase (1943). Assign different people to pantomime different actions. For example, how would Jack walk down a dusty road with two loaves of bread? How would Jack capture turkeys in his bag? How would Jack eat his supper? Have the people guess what actions each pantomimist is performing.

◄►

Sign Language

◄►

Learn signing to accompany a story you enjoy telling. Communicating with your usual storytelling habits is enhanced by the beauty of the hand signals. This idea might also include sharing stories with people who are deaf, who could also provide you with some help with sign language.

Check with your librarian for books dealing with sign language.

◄►

Hearing Magic

Start a log of words and phrases that are interesting, funny, dramatic, or musical. Collect proverbs, sayings, and speech usages that are unusual, pointed, or full of beauty. Not only will this be an enjoyable on-going activity, but the items collected can also be worked into stories later.

Interesting Words	Funny Words	Dramatic Words	Musical Words
cockamamie	oops	soaring	tinkling

Proverbs

    If you are patient in one moment of anger, you will escape one hundred days of sorrow. (Chinese)

Sayings

    It's raining cats and dogs.

Speech Usages

    ... so buck-teethed she could eat corn on the cob through a fence.

REFERENCES

Aranda, Charles. 1977. *Dichos: Proverbs and Sayings from the Spanish*. Santa Fe, N. Mex.: Sunstone.

Brown, Marcia. 1947. *Stone Soup: An Old Tale*. New York: Scribner.

Brunvand, Jan H. 1978. *The Study of American Folklore*. 2d ed. New York: W. W. Norton.

Chase, Richard. 1950. *Jack and the Three Sillies*. Boston: Houghton Mifflin.

Dickson, Paul. 1978. *The Official Rules*. New York: Delacourte.

Donaldson, Gerald. 1980. *Frogs*. New York: Van Nostrand Reinhold.

Hayes, Joe. 1982a. *Coyote and...*. Santa Fe, N. Mex.: Mariposa.

Livo, Norma J., and Sandra A. Rietz. 1986. *Storytelling: Process and Practice*. Littleton, Colo.: Libraries Unlimited.

Samskirti and Veda. 1977. *Hatha Yoga: Manual 1*. Honesdale, Pa.: The Himalayan International Institute of Yoga Science and Philosophy.

Wiesner, William. 1972. *Happy-Go-Lucky*. New York: Seabury.

4

Some Stories to Tell

INTRODUCTION

This chapter includes some stories and activities that belong in the area of folklore. Folklore can be defined as informal knowledge of a culture, usually orally transmitted, with its primary functions to educate and to entertain. The literature of the folk is, of course, part of folklore. Many of the participation suggestions given here also belong in the folklore category. The involvement of the listeners is a traditional aspect of oral societies.

MYTHOLOGY

More Dolphins

Diviner than the dolphin is nothing yet created: for indeed they were aforetime men....
(Greek origin)

To the dolphin alone, beyond all others, nature has granted what the best philosophers seek: friendship for no advantage. Though it has no need at all of any man, yet it is a genial friend to all and has helped many. (Plutarch, A.D. 46?-120)

Archaeologists recently discovered prehistoric images of a man swimming among dolphins. In Greek mythology, Apollo took the form of a dolphin and led a boat of Cretans to Delphi, the center of the world. For hundreds of years, Mediterranean seamen believed that a dolphin was a good omen and that, if their ship were lost, a dolphin would lead them home. A dolphin was considered an omen of good fortune sent by the gods to voyagers in ancient times.

Legends and myths about dolphins associating with humans have been a part of civilization for at least three thousand years. Arion, a Greek poet in the sixth century B.C. who was forced overboard, was saved by dolphins. The following story, "The Man on a Dolphin," is based on this event in which Arion, the greatest singer of tales of his time, was befriended by these amazing creatures.

"The Man on a Dolphin"*

◄►◄►◄►◄►◄►◄►◄►◄►◄►◄►◄►◄►◄►◄►◄►◄►◄►◄►

One time the bard, Arion, left Corinth, where he served in the court of Periander, for a tour of Sicily and Italy. Everywhere he was received with acclaim. His sea chest was filled with the treasures that were heaped on him at all the courts and from the contests he won. When at last it came time for him to return to Corinth, Arion went to the dock and sought out a Corinthian crew, for he felt he could trust them most of all the sailors on the sea. At last he found a Corinthian ship and booked passage.

On the day of departure, Arion came to the dock. He watched carefully as his chest was taken on ship and then he, too, went aboard. By the weight of the sea chest, the crew imagined the wealth it contained, and no sooner than they were on the high sea than the sailors plotted for the treasure. Arion was at the stern, sitting on his cargo, when he saw the crewmen menacingly approach.

"We will have your chest," their spokesman said. "And to be sure there is no accusation when we reach port, we will have your life now."

Arion raised himself as straight as could be.

"If you wish burial on land," said the spokesman, the crew drawing closer, "here is a dagger to kill yourself with, and we'll bury you when we land. Otherwise, you will throw yourself overboard without delay."

"When Arion saw his cause was useless, he slid off the chest and knelt before the sailors. "You may have the chest," he pleaded, "but let me keep my life!"

"And have you bring accusations when we land?" the seaman reasoned. "No. Here is the dagger and there is the sea. The choice is yours."

Arion said, "Then before I die, let me sing one last Orthian ode."

At that, the men were delighted. They would hear the greatest singer of tales in all the world, and they gave their consent. So Arion opened his sea

*In Harrell 1983. Reprinted by permission of John Harrell.

chest and dressed himself in the full costume of his calling. Then removing the kithara from the chest, he mounted the quarterdeck as his stage, and the men all assembled amidship. Arion began to sing, striding back and forth, his great voice carrying over the ship's deck and out to the open sea. When he had finished his performance at last, he flung himself grandly from the quarterdeck into the water. At the ship's side, the sailors watched as the ample costume spread out in the water and finally dragged Arion into the deep.

Now it happened that a dolphin had heard the voice of Arion and was enchanted. He had swam alongside the ship to hear his tale the better, so when Arion began to sink, the dolphin swam under him, lifted him up, and carried him to the port town of Taenarum. From there Arion journeyed on to Corinth in safety. Then he appeared before Periander and told him all that had happened. Periander thought Arion was just telling another story and had him confined until he learned the truth.

When the Corinthian ship came to port, Periander's guards summoned the crew to come before Periander.

"Have you had good fortune on your voyage?" Periander asked.

"Indeed we have," the spokesman replied.

"I believe you have returned from Italy," Periander pursued. "Can you give me word of Arion, for you know how favorable he is to me?"

"Yes, we saw him in Italy and he is there now, enjoying good health," the spokesman answered.

And then Arion appeared from behind a pillar, dressed as the crew last saw him. They could no longer hide their guilt, and the sea chest, with all its treasure, was returned.

From his wealth Arion commissioned an artist to make a bronze sculpture. It was on a man riding on a dolphin, and Arion placed the sculpture at the shrine in the port town of Taenarum as a tribute to the creature who had saved his life.

◀▶ ◀▶ ◀▶ ◀▶ ◀▶ ◀▶ ◀▶ ◀▶ ◀▶ ◀▶ ◀▶ ◀▶ ◀▶ ◀▶ ◀▶ ◀▶ ◀▶ ◀▶ ◀▶

This story of the interaction of a man and a dolphin seems too incredible to believe. Do dolphins know what they are doing when they help and sometimes save humans? Are they capable of feeling affection for particular humans? It is no more valid to refute these stories as mere folly than it is to accept them as obvious fact.

- Investigate other stories about dolphins and their contact with people.

- Tell or write a story from the first person point of view as if you had an encounter with a dolphin. How would you feel? What would you think? Share your story with others.

Myths

◀▶ ◀▶ ◀▶ ◀▶ ◀▶ ◀▶ ◀▶ ◀▶ ◀▶ ◀▶ ◀▶ ◀▶ ◀▶ ◀▶ ◀▶ ◀▶ ◀▶ ◀▶ ◀▶

Investigate myths as the encyclopedias of scientific information of preliterate societies. Myths are stories that tell how and why things are as they are. All folk groups had myths.

Classify and organize these stories into topics—creation, technology, morals, explanations of natural phenomena, etc.

Write an original explanation of a topic. For example, how might a member of a preliterate society explain the geysers in Yellowstone Park? Share these stories.

Develop a myth to explain where the wind comes from.

◀▶ ◀▶ ◀▶ ◀▶ ◀▶ ◀▶ ◀▶ ◀▶ ◀▶ ◀▶ ◀▶ ◀▶ ◀▶ ◀▶ ◀▶ ◀▶ ◀▶ ◀▶ ◀▶

FOLKLORE

A definition of folklore is informal knowledge of a culture, usually orally transmitted. Folklore has two primary functions: to educate and to entertain. Folklore is a process of the touch of the individual upon the culture. Even in today's high-technology culture, folklore is an ongoing process.

Create your own folklore magazine. Include in this magazine a title, a section for interviews of adults 65 years or older, and samples of local community folklore of the past. Some folklore of the past would include crafts, music, recipes, remedies, dances, stories (particularly ghost stories), idioms and sayings, superstitions, jokes, riddles, games, folk instruments, and customs dealing with marriage and death. The *Foxfire* collections are excellent examples of cultural journalism involving folklore.

Family Folklore

◄►◄►◄►◄►◄►◄►◄►◄►◄►◄►◄►◄►◄►◄►◄►◄►◄►◄►◄►

Consider some samples of the folklore of the present time. Folklore is developing continuously. Research the folklore of your family. What about your ancestry, family stories, origins of family names and traditions? Are there family reunions? If so, who brings what foods to the picnics? Is Aunt Virginia's cole slaw famous? Does she keep her recipe a secret? Tell about it. Did a member of your family fight in any wars? If so, which ones? What was his or her role in the war? Did anyone in your family live during the Great Depression? Collect any stories you can about it. Maybe some family members remember life in the dust bowl era. What can they tell you about it? Are there any stories of fortunes made or lost in your family? Were any of your family pioneers? (Pioneers still exist among us today. We all have chances to become pioneers.)

What will you do with your folklore magazine when you complete it? What will you name it? Copies of your magazine would make outstanding presents for family members and friends.

◄►◄►◄►◄►◄►◄►◄►◄►◄►◄►◄►◄►◄►◄►◄►◄►◄►◄►◄►

Rainbow Stories

Every culture has its own story or stories about how the rainbow came to be. The story of Noah and his ark, which includes how the rainbow came to be, is not limited to a single general cultural awareness. We now find references to the rainbow in greeting cards, wallpaper designs, cartoons, political statements, state lottery promotions, advertisements, and also language usage. The biblical story of Noah in Genesis culminates with the significance of the rainbow:

◄►◄►◄►◄►◄►◄►◄►◄►◄►◄►◄►◄►◄►◄►◄►◄►◄►◄►◄►

I do set my bow in the cloud and it shall be a token of a covenant between me and the earth.

And it shall come to pass, when I bring a cloud over the earth, that the bow shall be seen in the cloud:

And I will remember my covenant, which is between me and you and every living creature of all flesh; and the waters shall no more become a flood to destroy all flesh.

(Gen. 9: 13-15)

◄►◄►◄►◄►◄►◄►◄►◄►◄►◄►◄►◄►◄►◄►◄►◄►◄►◄►◄►

People have always felt the need to explain natural phenomena, and the rainbow, since it is so closely related to rain, has a great variety of explanations. For instance:

African:	The rainbow is a giant snake that comes out after a rainfall to graze.
African:	The rainbow is a sign that never again will the gods hold the rain and bring a drought that will kill the people.
Fon tribe, west African:	Treasure can be found where the rainbow ends.
Estonian:	The rainbow is the head of an ox, lowered to a river in drinking.
Ponca Indian:	The rainbow is really petals from the flowers.
Shoshoni Indian:	The rainbow is a giant serpent, who rubs his back on a dome of ice.
Finnish:	The rainbow is the sickle or bow of the Thunder God, whose arrow is the lightening.
North Asian:	The rainbow is a camel with three people on its back. The first beats a drum (thunder), the second waves a scarf (lightening), and the third pulls the reins, causing water (rain) to run from the camel's mouth.
Germanic:	The rainbow is the bowl God used at the time of the creation in tinting the birds.
Japanese:	The rainbow is the "Floating Bridge of Heaven."
Buddhists:	The colors of the rainbow were related to the seven planets and the seven regions of the earth.
Christians:	The rainbow's colors are sometimes linked to the seven sacraments.

The mythologies listed here about the rainbow are not all-inclusive. There are many other beliefs. Why are rainbows so popular world-wide? Why are there so many different versions as to the origins of the rainbow?

- Select one of the versions of how rainbows came to be and develop it into a story to tell.

- Are there any stories about a time in your life when you saw a rainbow? Was it special? If so, why? What do you remember? Tell about it.

A Trickster Swap

The trickster is a familiar character. He or she is an archetypal memory which takes the form of a person or animal in many folk literature traditions. The trickster is fox, coyote, raven, crow, spider, monkey, rabbit (Brer Rabbit), jackal, or human (Juan Bobo). The trickster often brings much good to mankind through cleverness and wisdom, but he or she is also credited with bringing misery, through deception and the making of tricks. The trickster is a clown, sometimes foolish, but never a fool. When the trickster does a good deed, even by accident, he or she is rewarded. But the trickster is also often selfish, falling victim to his or her own greed. Then, just as often, the punishment fits the crime. The trickster, deceiver, jester, mischief-maker, clever, quick-witted one and sometime visionary is a part of many cultural cosmologies. From such archetypal constructions, we learn history, mythology, and humanity.

Practiced storytellers might consider participating in a trickster swap, a telling-in-the-round of trickster/deception stories, with each teller presenting his or her favorite character and tale.

Suggestions

Coyote

"Coyote and the Crying Song" (Courlander 1970)

"Coyote and Locust" (Hayes 1982)

"Coyote Loses His Dinner" (Jones 1974)

"Coyote Steals a Blanket" (Robinson and Hill 1976)

"Coyote Steals the Summer" (Jones 1974)

"Coyote and the Rock" (Hayes 1982)

"Coyote and Rattlesnake" (Hayes 1982)

Crow

"The Crow and the Fox" (Green 1965)

"The Crow and the Serpent" (Korel 1964)

"The Crow and the Sparrow" (Spellman 1967)

"The Crow and the Whale" (Gilham 1943)

"The Crow in the Banyan Tree" (Gaer 1955)

Fox

"One Trick Too Many" (Ginsburg 1973)

"The Fox and the Geese" (De La Mare 1940)

"The Fox and the Lobster" (Carrick 1970)

"The Fox and the Peasant" (Ibid.)

"The Fox and the Rabbit" (Bowman and Bianco 1964)

"The Fox and the Rolling Pin" (Carey 1973)

"The Fox and the Sheepskin Jacket" (Arnott 1971)

"The Fox and the Thrush" (Ginsburg 1970)

"The Fox and the Quail" (Ginsburg 1973)

"A Fox in One Bite" (Scofield 1965)

"The Fox Turns a Somersault" (Hume 1962)

"A Fox Who Was Too Sly" (Pratt and Kula 1967)

Jackal

"The Jackal and the Bear" (Hitchcock 1966)

"The Jackal and the Crocodile" (Siddiqui and Lerch 1961)

"The Jackal Told Me" (Wyatt 1962)

"The Jackal and the Lambs" (Frobenius and Fox 1966)

"The Jackal and the Farmer" (Ibid.)

"The Jackal and the Hen" (Ibid.)

Juan Bobo

"Juan Bobo and the Old Tiger" (Jagendorf and Boggs 1960)

"Juan Bobo and the Cauldron" (Alegria 1969)

"Juan Bobo and the Princess Who Answered Riddles" (Ibid.)

Monkey

"The Monkey and Mr. Janel Sinna" (Tooze 1967)

"The Monkey and the Cat" (Aesop 1968)

"The Monkey and the Crocodile" (Babbit 1940)

"The Monkey and the Shark" (Montgomerie 1961)

"The Monkey and the Snail" (Dorliae 1970)

"The Monkey, the Tiger and the Jackal Family" (Siddiqui and Lerch 1961)

Rabbit

"Sheer Crops" (Botkin 1944)

"How Sandy Got His Meat" (Ibid.)

"The Wonderful Tarbaby Story" (Ibid.)

"Brer Dog and Brer Rabbit" (Ibid.)

"Rabbit Scratched the Elephant's Back" (Courlander and Prempeh 1957)

"Rabbit, Fox and the Rail Fence" (Ibid.)

"The Rabbit and the Tiger" (Alegria 1969)

"Rabbit and the Wolves" (Colwell 1976)

"The Rabbit Steals the Elephant's Dinner" (Burton 1962)

"The Rabbit Takes His Revenge on the Elephant" (Ibid.)

"The Rabbit Grows a Crop of Money" (Ibid.)

Raven

"Raven and the Keewak Bird" (Melzack 1970)

"Raven and the Goose" (Ibid.)

"Raven Fools His Grandchildren" (Maher 1969)

Spider

"Spider and Squirrel" (Arnott 1963)

"Spider and the Lion" (Ibid.)

"Spider Feeds His Family" (Arnott 1971)

"Anansi and Nothing Go Hunting for Wives" (Courlander 1947)

"Anansi and the Alligator Eggs" (Sherlock 1954)

"Anansi and the Elephant Exchange Knocks" (Courlander and Prempeh 1957)

"Anansi Hunts with Tiger" (Sherlock 1966)

"Anansi Plays Dead" (Courlander and Prempeh 1957)

"Anansi the Spider" (McDermott 1972)

"From Tiger to Anansi" (Johnson et al. 1977)

One specialization of a trickster swap might involve tellers in the exchanging of the same stories: the coyote version, the rabbit version, and the spider version of perhaps the story which tells how the trickster got all the stories. Try to locate all of the versions of "Sheer Crops" (Botkin 1944) which appear in the oral literatures of different cultures. Find all of the trickster stories in which the trickster tricks the gods, or those in which the trickster escapes death. Conduct a very specialized swap which uses these stories as its theme.

The African Storyteller

An African storyteller said that when one has traveled along a road he can sit down and wait for a story to overtake him. The story is like the wind. It comes from a far place and it can pass behind the back of a mountain.

"The Storyteller"*

◄►◄►◄►◄►◄►◄►◄►◄►◄►◄►◄►◄►◄►◄►◄►◄►◄►◄►◄►

Once in the land of Shoa, there was a king who loved nothing so much as listening to stories. Every moment of his time was spent listening to the tales told by the storytellers of his land, but there came a time when there were no stories that he had not heard.

His hunger for stories became known in the neighboring kingdoms and wandering singers and traveling storytellers came to Shoa to be rewarded for the new tales they could bring.

But the more tales the king heard, the fewer were left that he had not heard. Finally, in desperation he decreed that whatever storyteller could make him cry, "Enough! No more!" would be given a large part of his kingdom and the title of Ras, or prince.

Many people came to tell him stories, but he always sat and listened eagerly without ever protesting that he had heard too much. One day a farmer came and offered to tell the king stories until he would cry out, "Enough! No more!" The king just smiled at this.

"The best storytellers in Ethiopia have come and gone without telling me enough. You in your simple innocence to win the land and the title of Ras do not know what is ahead. Well, begin, you may try."

And so the humble farmer settled himself comfortably on a rug and began. "Once there was a peasant who sowed wheat. He mowed it when it was grown, threshed it, and put all the precious grain in his granary. It was a rich harvest. In fact, it was one of the best he had ever had. But, this is the

---

*Retold by Norma J. Livo from traditional material.

irony of the story. In his granary there was a tiny flaw. It was a hole big enough to pass a piece of straw through. And when the grain was all stored, an ant came and went through the hole and found the wheat. He carried away a single grain of it to his anthill to eat."

"Ah-ha! This is actually a story that I have never heard!" roared the king in delight.

"The next day, another ant came and carried away a grain."

"Ah-ha!"

"The next day still another ant came and carried away a grain."

"Yes, yes," interrupted the king. "I understand. Let us get on with the story."

"The next day another ant came and carried away another grain. And the next day another ant came and carried away another grain."

"Let us not dally with the details. The story is the thing," declared the king impatiently.

"The next day another ant came."

"Please, please," begged the king.

"But there are so many ants in this story. And the next day another ant came for a grain of wheat, and...."

"No, no! It must not be so!" demanded the king.

"Ah, but it is the crux of the story. And the next day another ant came and took away a grain...."

"But I understand all of this. Let us pass over it and get on with the plot," pleaded the king.

"And the next day another ant came and took his grain. And the next day...."

"Stop! I want no more of it!"

"The story must be told in the proper way," explained the farmer. "Besides the granary is still nearly full of wheat and it must be emptied. That is the story. And the next day...."

"No, no! Enough, enough!"

"And the next day another ant...."

"Enough, enough! You may have the land and the title of Ras!"

So the clever farmer became a prince and owned much land.

◀▶ ◀▶ ◀▶ ◀▶ ◀▶ ◀▶ ◀▶ ◀▶ ◀▶ ◀▶ ◀▶ ◀▶ ◀▶ ◀▶ ◀▶ ◀▶ ◀▶ ◀▶ ◀▶

This folk tale is a delightful example of a clever but powerless character winning out over a character holding the power. Many folk tales are based on this idea. Everyone roots for the little person's victory. Brer Rabbit and Coyote are several examples of powerless characters who use their cleverness to succeed in their dealings with those in power. Can you think of any other examples of this?

Create and tell a story using this idea.

Cumulative stories give listeners a chance to experience the repetitious building of a story and the playful predictability of language and story events. Young listeners can also become active participants in the story as they join in with the chant. A story such as *The Old Woman and Her Pig* (Jacobs 1892) allows for all of these possibilities.

Another activity might have children drawing pictures of the story characters on large poster boards. While a group of children reads the story as a chorus, the children with posters of the characters stand up, showing each poster when the character on it is mentioned. This provides more active involvement as well as a pictorial aid for memorization of the story.

There are several picture books, such as *Home before Midnight* (Lewis 1984) and *One Fine Day* (Hogrogian 1971), available with variants of this story. Use them for comparing and contrasting activities. How are they like *The Old Woman and Her Pig* and how are they different? *Home before Midnight* is a totally modern version yet the words are not changed at all. Sharing these two books, either through storytelling or examining the picture-story and reading aloud will be delightful extensions for this activity.

"The Old Woman and Her Pig"*

◄►

An old woman was sweeping her house, and she found a little crooked sixpence. "What," said she, "shall I do with this little sixpence? I will go to market, and buy a little pig."

As she was coming home, she came to a stile: but the piggy wouldn't go over the stile.

She went a little further, and she met a dog. So she said to him: "Dog! dog! bite pig; piggy won't go over the stile; and I shan't get home tonight." But the dog wouldn't.

She went a little further, and she met a stick. So she said: "Stick! stick! beat dog! dog won't bite pig; piggy won't get over the stile; and I shan't get home tonight." But the stick wouldn't.

She went a little further, and she met a fire. So she said: "Fire! fire! burn stick; stick won't beat dog; dog won't bite pig; piggy won't get over the stile; and I shan't get home tonight." But the fire wouldn't.

*In Jacobs 1892.

She went a little further, and she met some water. So she said: "Water! water! quench fire; fire won't burn stick; stick won't beat dog; dog won't bite pig; piggy won't get over the stile; and I shan't get home tonight." But the water wouldn't.

She went a little further, and she met an ox. So she said: "Ox! ox! drink water; water won't quench fire; fire won't burn stick; stick won't beat dog; dog won't bite pig; piggy won't get over the stile; and I shan't get home tonight." But the ox wouldn't.

She went a little further, and she met a butcher. So she said: "Butcher! butcher! kill ox; ox won't drink water; water won't quench fire; fire won't burn stick; stick won't beat dog; dog won't bite pig; piggy won't get over the stile; and I shan't get home tonight." But the butcher wouldn't.

She went a little further, and she met a rope. So she said: "Rope! rope! hang butcher; butcher won't kill ox; ox won't drink water; water won't quench fire; fire won't burn stick; stick won't beat dog; dog won't bite pig; piggy won't get over the stile; and I shan't get home tonight." But the rope wouldn't.

She went a little further, and she met a rat. So she said: "Rat! rat! gnaw rope; rope won't hang butcher; butcher won't kill ox; ox won't drink water; water won't quench fire; fire won't burn stick; stick won't beat dog; dog won't bite pig; piggy won't get over the stile; and I shan't get home tonight. But the rat wouldn't.

She went a little further, and she met a cat. So she said: "Cat! cat! kill rat; rat won't gnaw rope; rope won't hang butcher; butcher won't kill ox; ox won't drink water; water won't quench fire; fire won't burn stick; stick won't beat dog; dog won't bite pig; piggy won't get over the stile; and I shan't get home tonight." But the cat said to her, "If you will go to yonder cow, and fetch me a saucer of milk, I will kill the rat." So away went the old woman to the cow.

But the cow said to her: "If you will go to yonder haystack and fetch me a handful of hay, I'll give you the milk." So away went the old woman to the haystack; and she brought the hay to the cow.

As soon as the cow had eaten the hay, she gave the old woman the milk; and away she went with it in a saucer to the cat.

As soon as the cat had lapped up the milk, the cat began to kill the rat; the rat began to gnaw the rope; the rope began to hang the butcher; the butcher began to kill the ox; the ox began to drink the water; the water began to quench the fire; the fire began to burn the stick; the stick began to beat the dog; the dog began to bite the pig; the little pig in a fright jumped over the stile; and so the old woman got home that night."

◀▶ ◀▶ ◀▶ ◀▶ ◀▶ ◀▶ ◀▶ ◀▶ ◀▶ ◀▶ ◀▶ ◀▶ ◀▶ ◀▶ ◀▶ ◀▶ ◀▶ ◀▶ ◀▶

American Regional Stories

Read through some books on regional folk tales, such as the works of M. Jagendorf (all) and Philip D. Jordan (1957). Does your region have any familiar stories? Become a collector and seek out people who can share some of them with you.

For storyteller sources, contact local folklore or historical societies, state humanities programs, and anthropology or literature professors at local colleges and universities. Also look for potential storytellers among occupational groups such as miners, mill workers, farmers, cowboys, or loggers.

Tape and photograph the people who share their stories with you. Such a project could eventually result in a story/slide program for local social groups and schools, a cable TV production, or an anthology of local stories.

Variants

How many different variants can you find for the same story? Some of the old folk tales for which there are numerous versions are "Cinderella," "Rumplestiltskin," "Frog Princess," or "Fool of the World and the Flying Ship."

Photocopy the different story versions you find and start your own anthology of them. If a story is one you have heard, write it up and add it to your collection.

When you have a workable collection, study them to see how they are alike and how they are different. Create an adapted variant of your own to tell. Play with the details of setting and time in the story. For example, what would the story be like if told in the future (science fiction)?

Variations on a Theme

Objective: To develop fluency and flexibility in thinking.

"The Golden Thimble"*

◄►◄►◄►◄►◄►◄►◄►◄►◄►◄►◄►◄►◄►◄►◄►◄►◄►◄►◄►

In a little village lived a tiny woman who worked as a seamstress. All day long, until it grew too dark to see, she would sit at her window, sewing. Her work was beautiful, and people came from far away to admire it. When they asked her the secret of her craft, she would smile slyly and say, "The golden thimble, the golden thimble," and hold up her index finger to display her shining treasure. "A magician gave it to me when I was a girl. Thanks to my golden thimble, I can do what I do."

Years went by, and the woman grew old. Finally, she could no longer see well enough to work. All the maidens in the village yearned for the golden thimble, each one dreaming of the wonderful things she could make under its magical influence. At last the old woman decided to give her thimble to the woodcutter's beautiful daughter. The old seamstress handed the thimble to the young woman, kissed her gently, and said, "Guard it carefully. It is yours."

The woodcutter's daughter returned home with her precious gift and immediately sat down to work on her own wedding dress. But the stitches all came out crooked, the hem fell, and the laces, for some reason, would not lace. The maiden angrily went back to the old woman and threw the golden thimble in her lap. "It's no good!" she said. "It doesn't work!" And she told the old seamstress what had happened.

The old seamstress listened carefully to the maiden's story. Then she looked shrewdly at the woodcutter's daughter and said, "Of course it didn't work for you. You're an idiot."

◄►◄►◄►◄►◄►◄►◄►◄►◄►◄►◄►◄►◄►◄►◄►◄►◄►◄►◄►

"The Golden Thimble" has two main characters, an old woman and a beautiful, young woman. The ingredients of the plot include: people came from far away to admire the old woman's sewing; her secret—the golden thimble, which she got from a magician; the old woman gave the thimble to the young woman; the young woman's stitching was a failure; she returned the thimble to the old woman in anger; and finally, the old woman's reply.

---

*In Harris 1986, 32-33. Reprinted by permission of John Harris.

How many different variations of this story can you develop?

- Who are your characters going to be?

- What did your first character do exceedingly well?

- Who else could have some magical object?

- Where did he or she get the magical object?

- What did the magical object help the first character do?

- Describe the person, the work, the setting.

- Who did the first character give the magical object to? Why?

- How did it work for the second character?

- How did that person return the magical object?

- What was the final reply?

Have each person in a group develop his or her own variation of "The Golden Thimble" and tell it to the group.

Stringing Stories Together

Frontier stories, especially whoppers and one-liners, tend to cluster by topic: stories about wind, trains, twisters, sheep, fish, mosquitoes, or rain storms. Such stories invite the construction of a longer monologue consisting of several shorter pieces strung together (Livo and Rietz 1986, 166-68). Collections of short stories and whoppers can provide an ample supply: *A Treasury of American Folklore* (Botkin 1944); *A Treasury of Western Folklore* (Botkin 1951); *Whoppers, Tall Tales and Other Lies* (Schwartz 1975); and *America's 101 Most High Falutin', Big Talkin', Knee Slappin' Gollywhoppers and Tall Tales: The Best of the Burlington Liar's Club* (Diendorfer 1980).

Consider chaining a series of mosquito stories together using common liar's interchange: "Why, I remember one time.... And then there was this.... But none 'o that can stand against the time that...."

If you are a more practiced teller, you might give each individual in a group a collection of six to ten short stories and lies about specific items or topics. One person might have a handful of stories about the heat ("It was sooo hot that ... HOW HOT WAS IT?"). Another might have wind stories. Still another might have crop stories, insect stories, or fish stories. Have each story-teller then construct a monologue by combining some or all of the given items—pigs, sheep, cows, corn, dogs, horses, barns, GUMBO....

What Would You Do with These?

The Gumbo was so deep that when I got stuck in it last spring, I had to go back up to the house to get a rope to pull myself out.

I saw a cowpoke sittin' in the middle of a mess of gumbo one time, asked him if he needed a ride. He said I was to be thanked kindly all the same, but that he had a perfectly good horse under him.

One year, the gumbo was so bad that it caked and dried 'round the tails of the pigs when they kicked it up walkin'. Got so heavy, it stretched their skins back so far they couldn't close their eyes. Whole lot died of insomnia.

What Would You Do with THESE?

We had very little wind here in Texas last year. I have three windmills on my ranch, and there was so little wind that I had to take two of them down to get enough wind to run the other one. The funny thing is, if I hadn't taken down the barbed wire fence that was holding up most of the wind, I don't think that third windmill would have worked either.

(Diendorfer 1980)

Up here in Alberta, we really have some wind storms. Last summer a rancher had just finished digging 2,000 post holes when up came a nor'wester and blew those postholes clean out of the ground. When found 125 miles away they were a total loss—so full of holes from bounding over the cactus that they wouldn't hold dirt anymore.

(Diendorfer 1980)

In South Dakota this is the way the wind blows. When we are starting out to plow a field, we always mark off the headlands first. Then we head down through the field—the same way the wind is blowing—go a little way, throw the plow on the ground and go back and start on the next furrow. We don't bother going all the way—after a row is started. The wind is so strong it will blow the furrow right through to the other end of the field.

(Diendorfer 1980)

Or These?

The melons in Texas grow fairly big. Any melon that doesn't weight 50 pounds is fed to the hogs. One year a melon grew so big that it had to be carried to market on a flatcar. It wasn't so bad that the field level sunk two feet from the weight of the melon. But it was awful when they opened it up and the juice flooded two counties.

(Diendorfer 1980)

My uncle Egbert, who lives in Kentucky, raised a watermelon so big he hauled it to a country fair, hammered a spigot in the side and sold watermelon juice for a week. Then he cracked it open and sold watermelon for the last 11 days of the fair. What made him mad is that the fair didn't last long enough—and half the melon went to waste.

(Diendorfer 1980)

A man living west of town here tried to raise watermelon this summer. He had very bad luck. The soil was too rich. The watermelon vines grew so fast that they wore the watermelons out, draggin' them along the ground. One of the boys from town went out to swipe a melon. He got a melon, all right, but the vines were growing so fast that warm night that the boy had to be taken to the hospital. It seems before he could break that melon off the vine, it had dragged him half a mile, and he was in bad shape.

(Diendorfer 1980)

Nursery Rhymes

◄►

Familiar nursery rhymes are excellent material for finger play activities. Seat a group of children in a circle. Go around the circle and recite as many nursery rhymes as the children can remember. After demonstrating how finger play enhances several of these, have the children select a nursery rhyme and invent finger play motions to go with it. Then have them share with the group.

Little Miss Muffet

Little Miss Muffet sat on a tuffet
[Fist with thumb standing.]

Eating her curds and whey.
[Pretend to eat.]

Along came a spider
[Running motion with fingers.]

And sat down beside her
["Spider" sits beside "tuffet."]

And frightened Miss Muffet away.
[Throw hands out.]

Jack and Jill

Jack and Jill went up the hill
[Fists clenched, thumbs erect, move in ascending motion.]

To fetch a pail of water.
[Motion continued.]

Jack fell down
[Fist clenched, thumb pointing down, moves in whirling, descend-
    ing motion.]

And broke his crown
[Motion continued.]

And Jill came tumbling after.

Up Jack jumped and said to Jill
[Fists clenched, one thumb erect.]

As in his arms he took her
[Two thumbs approach each other.]

"Let's get that pail of water."

So up the hill went Jack and Jill
[Fists clenched, thumbs erect, move in ascending motion.]

And got that pail of water,
[Motion continued.]

And brought it down to mother dear,
[Fists clenched, thumbs erect, move in descending motion.]

Who thanked her son and daughter:

"Thank you, Jack! Thank you, Jill."
[Right thumb makes bow; left thumb makes bow.]

◄►◄►◄►◄►◄►◄►◄►◄►◄►◄►◄►◄►◄►◄►◄►◄►◄►◄►◄►

FAMILY HISTORY

Performing Family History

Preservation of an oral literature is an interesting problem that many human cultures have solved in essentially the same manner by passing on stories from one live storyteller to another and relying upon human memory for accuracy of transmission. Even with newer technologies, preservation remains as problematic as ever. Print cannot encode oral language or the many paralinguistic elements that are invested in the oral story. Audio tape recording loses the visual charm and power of the oral story. Video tape, while it preserves visual elements, freezes one telling, disallowing the natural process of change that would otherwise occur in the live setting.

Individuals wishing to save the stories told by older family members face essentially the same options for preservation and technological restrictions that folklorists face. Transcriptions encode the stories into written language, losing the essence of the oral language "character" of the material. Audio tapes preserve sound, but lose the visual effect of the stories. Video taping may be the best means for keeping the physical essence and style of the teller in memory, but even this medium is limiting. A growing number of storytellers are turning to another, older method — preservation through live performance.

In the habit of many oral literatures, modern storytellers are learning to do (usually) first-person tellings of the stories of their older relatives, of friends, of their cultures' histories, and of archetypal men and women within their cultures. The best of these cast the experiences of many individuals into the character of one person. This one becomes an archetypal, almost mythical representative of all who lived out a set of circumstances, like, for example, the pioneer woman. But the most fruitful approach, perhaps, for the individual who would like to simply collect and keep alive the recollections of an uncle, mother, or grandfather is the intimate, first-person telling.

Familiarity with the language and body language habits of the individual whose stories are to be retold can be built through conversation, tapings, study of video materials, and oral transcriptions. The "slotting" of content into structure that is the process of the oral telling is more restricted for such renditions because the storyteller is taking on the character and behavior — as well as the story — of another storyteller. The teller cannot tell the material as he or she would tell it, but as someone else would tell it.

The following story is only one of many collected and told by Elnor Knutson of Helena, Montana. Elnor takes on the character of her own grandmother for the telling. Her specialty is the story told from the point of view of her grandmother at the age of five or six years. By choosing in some stories to portray her grandmother as a child, Elnor manages to recount the history of six generations: her grandmother's grandmother and mother, her grandmother, her mother, herself, and her own children.

Sudie and the Wagon Trains*

◄►◄►◄►◄►◄►◄►◄►◄►◄►◄►◄►◄►◄►◄►◄►◄►◄►◄►◄►

This story is taken from stories told to me by my grandmother as we sat outside on a lazy summer afternoon, sharing and swapping memories. My grandmother's name is Sudie Lancaster; she lives in Pueblo, Colorado. This story took place when she was five or six years of age, when she and her family lived on the Texas-Oklahoma border near a wagon trail.

"Get your bones all settled comfortable, because it is such a nice afternoon for sitting and remembering."

"Do you really want to sit with me?" my grandmother asked as we settled down on the porch in our own rockers.

"Grandma, what was it like when you were just a youngin'?"

"Well, I remember one time my mother spit through a keyhole and hit me right in the eye. It sure splatted. I'll never forget the sound it made or the icky feeling it gave me."

"Could you please tell me about what brought that on?"

"Well, I couldn't just give you that without telling you some things that went along with it. It goes back to the time when I was just five or six. We lived near the wagon trail. Daddy used to be a peace officer and was gone most of the time, so what Maw said, went!"

"When it came garden time, we had to do what Maw said or else! I can remember just as clear as day how Maw used to say, 'SUUUDIEEEEEE ... don't you go gettin' the citron and watermelon seeds mixed up. You know we have to plant the citron on the outside of the garden and the watermelon on the inside of the garden, because of the people in the wagon trains a-helpin' themselves.' Citron is only good for making watermelon pickles and is not fit to eat. 'SUUUDIEEEEEE ... get the water buckets and your brother and get some water up to the house. The train is comin' and the water will not be clear again for almost two days.' We had to haul enough for cookin' and drinkin' before a train came through or go without. 'SUUUDIEEEEEE ... you get that dog out of the garden right now!' You should have seen the get-up my brother fixed for the dog for waterin' the garden. He made a harness, so we could put four lard pails full of water on the dog. Then we would chase him through the garden. The dog would slosh and spill the water; then we wouldn't have to do the waterin' ourselves."

"Maw would get lonesome with Dad gone so much, so she would often invite some of the women from a wagon train in to tea. She would close the

---

*Used by permission of Elnor Knutson.

door to keep out the dog and the chickens and make us kids go outside, so she could talk in peace and in private. I never could resist temptation; I would always peek through the keyhole to see what was a-goin' on. 'SUUUDIEEEEEE ... I'm warnin' you, now. Someday you're gonna learn not to go spyin' on folks through keyholes!' One time she had company. I just couldn't stop myself. I had to look in at the keyhole. Maw took aim and let go with a wad of chewin' tobacco, and it hit me right in the eye. I didn't look through the keyhole no more ... for about a week. You see, women in the South often smoked a corncob pipe or chewed tobacco. That's how it was when I was a kid. I remember Maw spitting through the keyhole more than once. But that's the only time she ever got me in the eye."

Then Grandmother ended her rememberin' for a spell and took a snooze in the chair. We spent many an afternoon bringing up memories of days long gone, one recollection at a time. Grandmother was not as spry as she had been before she turned 100.

◀▶ ◀▶ ◀▶ ◀▶ ◀▶ ◀▶ ◀▶ ◀▶ ◀▶ ◀▶ ◀▶ ◀▶ ◀▶ ◀▶ ◀▶ ◀▶ ◀▶ ◀▶ ◀▶

Some first-person history tellers wear full costume for performance, some only bits and pieces; some make no effort to change their own physical appearances. Since the essence of the telling is the story and not the storyteller—we do not "see" the storyteller, only the story—elaborate costuming and trim should not be necessary.

Circle Swap of Personal History or Experience

We all share experiences that center about standard circumstances: camping, traveling in the car (as a child or with children), having company for dinner disasters. Rounds of swapping of such related topic tales are common and occur frequently, without the usual, more formal trappings of the official storytelling. Many of us have participated in anecdotal exchanges, telling plane stories, conference stories, pregnancy stories, dog stories, husband or wife stories, parent stories, kid stories. Such rounds of storying just happen. No one says, "Hey, let's all tell about the times when...."

The following starters, by no means representing all such possibilities, could lead to a spontaneous round of swapping of personal stories.

1. When I was a kid, we used to go to _____[name]_____ every summer. One time _____

2. One time, I planned this dinner for a [name/s] and _____

3. The last time I really became frightened on a plane (flight) was when _____

4. Traveling with the kids and the dog is something that has to be endured. I remember when _____

5. I once had a pet _____[name]_____ that _____
   One time it _____

Such personal stories often bring the most pleasure. Everyone is the storyteller, and all experience the confirmation of commonality of circumstance and of community that is the hallmark of the close cultural experience with the oral literature.

Do you have one to go along with these?

A Personal Anecdote

◄►◄►◄►◄►◄►◄►◄►◄►◄►◄►◄►◄►◄►◄►◄►◄►◄►◄►◄►

When I was a kid, we used to camp in schoolyards or public parks in the small towns in the west. There were no campgrounds then, and motels, such as they were, charged two or three dollars per night per family. "Entirely too much!" Father would declare. So we hauled a one-wheeled trailer along behind a 1947 Ford and packed canvas water bags up front, hooked over the radiator. One night, somewhere in the middle of Kansas, a tornado blew up. Since this was not familiar weather, Kansas not being our territory, we didn't react quickly enough. The tent was pitched; we were all settled in, and the wind began to screech. The tent pole—the tent was a four-corner, center post, olive drab, army surplus affair that weighed a good 40 pounds dry—began to shift and dance. Then it hopped clean off the ground, not once but again and again, each time a bit higher. Dad was quick in the face of trouble. "Grab the pole!" he yelled. We all hung onto the pole as it pitched and heaved, pulling us up off the ground at each bounce. I don't know how long this went on. Longer than we thought was necessary for the purposes of instruction. Then the wind died, the tent settled and sagged. Mother and Dad went out to repeg and retie loose ends. That's when they discovered the unlocked tornado cellar alongside the schoolhouse—the schoolhouse which, as providence would have it, stood between the tent, the car, the trailer and the full velocity of the wind.

* * *

When I was a kid, I wanted a garden. I saw my parents make a garden every year, so I wanted one, too. Mom and Dad offered me my choice of seed packages and bedding plants, but, no. I wanted a garden with yellow flowers in it, just like the yellow flowers in the lawn. Yellow was my favorite color. "Here," said Dad, handing me the dandelion digger. "Go dig 'em up, and we'll plant them right here in a row." He dug a row, while I tenderly lifted one dandelion after another from the lawn. I planted and watered my little crop with care, but all of the dandelions died. "Why?" I wanted to know. "Didn't get enough root system," was the absolutely correct reply. "Here." And I took the digger, determined to get more root system. But to no avail. My second planting died. And my third, fourth, and fifth. I was digging dandelions from the alley, the neighbor's side yard, and the city easement next to the street. My supply was dwindling; I was desperate. "More root system!" Dad would say, hand me the digger, and smile.

* * *

In the west, especially on a clear day, distant mountains loom large. They might be just across the street. Size is difficult to assess and distance is deceiving. One time Dad decided that we could drive from Colorado Springs to the top of Pikes Peak and back before breakfast. We all believed him; he believed himself. We had a very, very, very late breakfast.

◄► ◄► ◄► ◄► ◄► ◄► ◄► ◄► ◄► ◄► ◄► ◄► ◄► ◄► ◄► ◄► ◄► ◄► ◄► ◄►

Memories

◄► ◄► ◄► ◄► ◄► ◄► ◄► ◄► ◄► ◄► ◄► ◄► ◄► ◄► ◄► ◄► ◄► ◄► ◄► ◄►

The Family Folklore Program, established in 1974, was part of the Smithsonian Institution's annual Festival of American Folklife. They made available photos scavenged from secondhand shops and drew a steady stream of visitors from the first day on. They interviewed people (the interviewers were mostly graduate students in the Department of Folklore and Folklife at the University of Pennsylvania) in open-ended, individual sessions. The interviewers were armed with a long list of questions from which to choose. The interviews were taped and one of the results was *A Celebration of American Family Folklore* by Steven J. Zeitlin, Amy J. Kotkin, and Holly Cutting Baker (1982). The photographs had opened the floodgates of personal memories and associated feelings.

Collect a large quantity of old family photographs and make them available for the participants. Spread them out in the room and ask everyone to pick out one of the photographs that reminds them of something in their own life. Have them move around the room and share with other people what memories their chosen photograph evokes.

◄► ◄► ◄► ◄► ◄► ◄► ◄► ◄► ◄► ◄► ◄► ◄► ◄► ◄► ◄► ◄► ◄► ◄► ◄► ◄►

My Most Embarrassing Moment

◄►◄►◄►◄►◄►◄►◄►◄►◄►◄►◄►◄►◄►◄►◄►◄►◄►◄►◄►

Ask each person to think about his or her most embarrassing moment — we all have them! Have them share these moments in small groups. Have the people then select a story from their group as the "winner" and share these winners with the large group.

Did the winning stories change in any way when they were told to the whole group? If so, why was this?

◄►◄►◄►◄►◄►◄►◄►◄►◄►◄►◄►◄►◄►◄►◄►◄►◄►◄►◄►

Yesterday

◄►◄►◄►◄►◄►◄►◄►◄►◄►◄►◄►◄►◄►◄►◄►◄►◄►◄►◄►

If there is one thing that we all have in common, it is that we have all experienced "yesterday." That is where commonality ends. Each of our "yesterdays" are unique to each of us. Even if we shared some of the time involved in "yesterday," our perceptions and experiences are still totally unlike anyone else's.

"Yesterday" is part of everyone's individual history. It sometimes helps to review that history and share how it differs and how it is like the "yesterday" of others. On days of national trauma (such as the Challenger tragedy or the assassination of a national hero), we all can remember where we were when we heard the news, how others around us reacted to it, and how we felt. Our common and usual "yesterday" also holds special moments for us.

Have everyone get in pairs. Ask each person to share three things or scenes from his or her yesterday. After people have done this, have them organize and write a story which could be added to their storytelling journal. The story might have a title such as "My Special Yesterday" or "My Unusual Yesterday."

◄►◄►◄►◄►◄►◄►◄►◄►◄►◄►◄►◄►◄►◄►◄►◄►◄►◄►◄►

PARTICIPATION STORIES

Many times listeners become active participants in a story. Participation gives the story to the audience; it brings an audience into the story. Opportunities for such involvement come naturally when stories contain repeated refrains, chants, songs, rhymes, or chances for movement, noise-making, or clapping.

Find a story that provides opportunities for audience participation or invest a story that does not already have them with such participation spots. Prepare the story for telling and try it out on a real audience.

Did it work?

What would you change?

What would you add?

What would you remove?

Tailoring a Story—Participation

Perhaps because the oral language is accessible to all who can speak it, and because the oral stories, with their generic structures and recognizable archetypes, belong to collective communities, people often assume that the told story is group property. The storytelling is not, after all, a performance given by one individual, but a story building conducted by a storyteller on behalf of the audience who owns the material. The teller is the property of the story and of the audience during the telling. The teller extends story ownership to the audience.

Allowing the audience to assume control of the story is not always an easy and automatic operation. Today's audiences often don't know the story, and therefore don't know how and when to "come in." In addition, they are so schooled in proper audience behavior for performance, that they may feel constrained not to "interrupt." And, since audience interaction is generally not coded into written transcriptions of stories, the storyteller is given few, if any, cues as to how an audience might participate.

In order to extend story ownership to an audience through participation, the storyteller must find a story that can "take" overt audience participation, determine the nature of that participation, work the participation device or devices into the story, then teach/cue the audience to its part.

Some of the best remembered participation stories are camp materials: "Going on a Bear/ Lion Hunt," "Little Bunny Foo Foo," "Herman the Worm," and "The Coughin' Coffin." These tales are almost "cult" material, so universal in the oral transmission of childhood literature that everyone knows them and can join in. As with such songs as "She'll Be Comin' 'round the Mountain," the audience understands its part. In the case of the "melodrama type" of story, the audience may not know the story content, but certainly understands its role in cheering, booing, and other noisemaking. Such story participations need no instruction and little cuing from the storyteller. (These stories may be the remnants, in our own culture and time, of the traditional storytelling, in which the audience knew the stories as well as the teller and automatically did its part. The repetition of stories implicit in traditional practice did not bore the audience. Rather, audiences delighted in helping to tell stories that they already knew.)

Today's storyteller can tailor a story to include audience participation through movement, clapping, chanting, singing, and general noisemaking.

1. TALKING — Numerous stories contain clues to audience participation in their titles. For instance, "The Talking Boat" (Cimino 1970), "The Talking House" (Heady 1965), "The Talking Fish" (Tashjian 1966), and "The Talking Pot" (Hatch 1947) all contain language sequences that can be talked, chanted, or sung by the audience. The storyteller need only extend the opportunity. Other stories, especially cumulative stories that wind and unwind, contain repetitions language sequences which the audience may repeat along with the teller. For a taxing and challenging exercise, try "The Tabby Who Was Such a Glutton" (Asbjornsen and Moe 1960).

2. SHOUTING — Counting sequences, stories in which characters speak one- or two-word lines, and those in which special sound effects are to be made will allow the audience a chance to make some noise. If, for instance, a story calls for a character to say, "Who's there?" as in "One Trick Too Many" (Ginsburg 1973), the audience can easily learn to say that line. Should groups of people in a story say, "AHHHHH," or "NOOOOOOO," the audience can be assigned these parts.

3. QUESTION/ANSWER — Audiences can take the part of an echo, ask a question, or give an answer. In "The Flea" (Saltman 1985), one story section (which would require some expansion) provides an example of an echo sequence.

   (The beetle cues the shepherd about what to demand of the king.)

   "I would like a cart to ride home in," said the beetle.
   "I would like a cart to ride home in," said the shepherd.

   "And two oxen to drive it," said the beetle.
   "And two oxen to drive it," said the shepherd.

   "And a load of corn in it," said the beetle.
   "And a load of corn in it," said the shepherd.

   "And two fine horses to tie on behind it," said the beetle.
   "And two fine horses to tie on behind it," said the shepherd.

   (Saltman 1985)

In "The Fisherman and His Wife" (Johnson et al. 1977), the fish asks a repeat question that the audience can easily do, while "The Talking Pot" uses a question/answer device that will allow the storyteller to ask the audience the question and the audience to chant the answer.

> "I skip! I skip!" said the pot.
> "How far will you skip?" asked the woman.
> "Up the hill and down the dale and into the rich man's house!"
>   cried the little pot.

(Hatch 1947)

4. NOISEMAKING — Audiences can be encouraged to cry, laugh, moo, cluck, and otherwise add sound effects to a story. Hand signals can be used by the storyteller to cue specific responses. Stories that contain noise "words" are a special delight, especially if the audience can say the "noises." "Why Mosquitoes Buzz in People's Ears" (Aardema 1975) contains such wonderful noises as "WASAWUSU WASAWUSU," "KILLEE WILLEE," "KRIK KRIK" and "MEK MEK." "Who's in Rabbit's House?" (Aardema 1977), has such as "GDUNG GDUNG," "KOK KOK KOK," "GUMM GUMM," "KAPITA KAPITA," "DILAK DILAK DILAK," and "GNISH," all ready-made for audience involvement. The storyteller can add physical noisemaking to the story line by looking for it in the narration. Audiences can clap, snap fingers, slap knees, stomp feet, rub hands together, snore, grunt and groan, or blow like the north wind. The story, itself, will provide direction.

5. MOVEMENT — The storyteller can plan natural and invented movement for the audience to do during the storytelling. Natural movement — body language — can be cued when a story character moves in a common manner: shrugging, grinning, nodding, etc. Invented movement — somewhat more theatrical — can be inserted where appropriate. For instance, the audience might be instructed to throw their arms into the air each time the talking pot says, "I skip!" or to rock or lean with the blowing of the wind. If a given character says, "Oh me! Oh dearie, dearie me! And what shall I do now?" the audience can feign exaggerated despair, either by wringing hands or by holding their arms to their bowed heads in the melodramatic "oh woe" position.

Movements of the audience can grow easily and naturally from a storyteller's applied paralinguistic effects. The storyteller can simply examine some of the movements and postures that he or she employs during the telling of a given story, then consider methods for extending these to the audience. Such audience movement is cued by the teller with no signal other than the telling of the story itself. The audience follows the storyteller.

Letting the Audience Decide

Audiences that hear stories more than once are in a position to think critically about adding various participation devices to a particular bit of material. Classroom teachers might use a familiar story as an exercise in critical thinking/problem solving during which the students plan, add, try out, and critique the workability of invented effects. Teachers of storytellers might try the same exercise to help prospective tellers learn how to examine, modify, and tailor a story for audience participation.

While some stories do not lend themselves to such manipulation, many more do. The purist might object to tampering with a story on the grounds that we can't know which effects properly belong. On the other hand, sufficient anthropological evidence suggests that audiences participate enthusiastically throughout a storytelling, sometimes singing, dancing, and acting out in spontaneous fashion, while the teller goes right on. Though we may not know the precise "how" of participation for transcribed stories, we can be sure that participation was a fact for this material. Providing an opportunity for audience participation that is in keeping with and that is even cued by story narrative seems less of an offense against tradition than performances which eliminate it altogether.

Percussion Stories

Pounding and making noise, random or orderly, is a very satisfying thing to do. Watch the adult join with a preschooler in a fulfilling round of banging on pots, pans, lids, and jars with the kitchen's offering of wooden spoons. And who is having the better time? Adults have formalized this kind of play and attributed great status to it, e.g., the drummer in a band, any kind of band. But all of these activities which recast adult pounding and banging as sophisticated do not really conceal the ecstasy to be captured in the simple act of beating out noise. Make a joyful sound. And what else, as an adult excuse for exercising wild abandon, could be more joyful? Perhaps it is not the sound that is joyful, after all, but the rush of pleasure gained from making it.

Consider telling a "pot and pan" story, in which drummings on kitchen hand-me-downs provide a steady cadence and "voice" for much of the activity in the event sequence. The following story is given in its entirety as retold by this author, with (*) markings given in the text at insertion points for various punctuations of poundings, thrummings, and pitter-patterings and italicizing indicating an undercurrent of noise. Listen for possibilities for noisemaking suggested in the narration. Everyone's own kitchenware collection will determine the nature and range of choice available. (Italicized sections indicate drumming, etc., to accompany narration.)

"The Fox and the Quail"*

◀▶ ◀▶ ◀▶ ◀▶ ◀▶ ◀▶ ◀▶ ◀▶ ◀▶ ◀▶ ◀▶ ◀▶ ◀▶ ◀▶ ◀▶ ◀▶ ◀▶ ◀▶

One day, *Fox was walking along when he heard* a voice. * *It rumbled and grumbled and complained.* "Who's there?" said Fox. "I'm here," said his stomach, * for it was indeed his stomach. "Where are you?" said Fox, looking around, up and down. "I'm right here," said the voice. * *"And it's time that you paid me some mind. Do you know how long I've waited for a decent meal?" Fox trotted off at a good pace, taking his stomach with him, thinking to find it a meal.*

He came to Quail's tree and pounded upon the trunk with his paw. * The echo resounded and carried up the length of the hollow trunk * to the place where Quail sat guarding her babies. *Her heart began to pound. "Who's there?" she called down.* "It is I, Fox," said Fox. *"My stomach tells me that it is hungry. You will find something to fill it or I will have to climb up there and eat you and your babies."*

Quail flew down from her nest * and sat next to Fox on the ground, but not too close. "Very well," she said. "I will find something for you to eat, but you must promise to do exactly as I say." "I will! I will!" Fox promised. *Quail then flew along the path; Fox followed close behind. When they came to the village road, Quail ordered Fox to hide behind a nearby bush.* She remained sitting in the center of the road. Before long, a buggy came rolling lightly along. * *An old woman and her granddaughter sat side by side in the seat, the woman clucking to a slow old horse as they moved down the road. Behind them on a cloth-covered platter sat a tall stack of steaming buttered pancakes, and next to these, a crock of honey.*

Quail began to flutter lamely in the road in front of the buggy. * "Oh! Look, Grandmother!" said the girl. "A bird with a broken wing. * I had better go catch it and help it to mend." The girl hopped out of the buggy despite her grandmother's protests. "Child, don't go. It's an old trick. The bird is not lame. It probably has a nest nearby and wants to lead us away." But the girl did not listen. *Quail flopped and fluttered off into the nearby field, thence to the woods beyond, while the girl gave chase. The grandmother came along behind, puffing, hobbling with difficulty, and all the while, calling for the girl to come back.* Fox put his paw over his face to keep from chuckling and giving himself away. * And when the grandmother, too, disappeared into the forest, Fox came out from his hiding place, climbed into the buggy and ate all of the buttery pancakes smothered in honey.

Quail went home to guard her babies. Fox could no longer hear his stomach. *As he walked slowly and heavily along the road, he heard another voice.* "You!" it said. * "Who?" said Fox. * "Me!" said the voice. * "Your

---

*Adapted from Ginsburg 1973.

throat!" it said, for the voice was indeed that of his throat. * "Where?" said Fox. "Here!" said the voice. * "I'm thirsty!" it said. * *"You can't expect me to put down such a load of pancakes and honey without giving me something to drink."*

Off Fox trotted, until he came to Quail's tree. He pounded upon the trunk with his paw. * *"Who is it?" said Quail, her heart pounding.* "It is I, Fox," said Fox. *"What do you want this time, Fox?"* * "My throat complains of thirst, Quail," said Fox. * "Find me something to drink or I shall have to climb the tree and eat you and your babies." *Quail flew down to sit beside Fox, but not too close.* "I found food for you when you were hungry," she said. "It should be enough, but, very well, and only on the condition that you do as I say."

Quail flew down the path. Fox came along close behind. Once again, Quail led Fox to the village road, and, once again, she ordered him to hide. * *In a short time a wagon lumbered along the road. It was heavy timbered and it bore a heavy load — the village burgermeister and a full cask of beer. It creaked and rattled as it came. When it reached Quail, she flew up to perch upon the burgermeister's head.* "Donnerwetter!" he mumbled, and he brushed her away. * She then settled on his shoulder, * digging in her claws. "Noch ein mal!" and * he slapped at her, but missed. *She circled about to alight on the horse's tail.* "Donnerwetter, noch ein mal!" The man reached for her, * and lost both his balance and his temper. * She flew around his head several times, then * landed on the cask of beer. He picked up the axe which he always kept nearby, and heedless of all consequences, * brought it down on the barrel. When the barrel split open, * *and the beer began to pour into the wagon bed, he roared impolitely* and chased Quail across the field and into the forest, waving the axe over his head. *

* Fox could barely control his mirth, but kept his paw over his face. When the burgermeister disappeared, Fox climbed into the wagon and drank all of the beer. * *As he rambled away, he felt rather light headed and he heard a giggle.* * "Who's that?" asked Fox. "Just me, or rather, just you," giggled the giggle. * "Who is me?" asked Fox. * "I'm the you in your head," said the giggle, * for it was indeed Fox's mind. "You haven't laughed or been well entertained in a long time. I'm ready for fun!" said the giggle. Find me some fun!"

Fox trotted back to Quail's tree and pounded on the trunk with his paw. The noise resounded in the hollow of the tree, and Quail's heart pounded. "Who's there?" she asked. "Fox," giggled Fox. "I need some good laughs," said Fox. "Find me some entertainment, or I will have to climb the tree and eat you and your babies."

Quail flew to the base of the tree. * She sat beside Fox, but not too close. "I found food for you when you were hungry and drink when you were thirsty, Fox. It should be enough." * "Not enough," giggled Fox. "Then follow," said Quail, "but do as I say." *Quail flew down the path. Fox kept close, but stumbled often. Soon the path narrowed, then became a thin track, then little more than bent grass marked a way. Quail flew until she* *came to a rude cabin in a small clearing. She ordered Fox to hide.* He did, and * looking out from behind a rock, he saw a poor shack with a bit of a sagging porch. On that porch sat an old man and an old woman. They had very little. They wore patched, thin clothing and bark pieced together for shoes. As they sat, the old man twisted grass into rope, * and the old woman churned milk to make butter. * *Quail flew up to sit upon the old woman's shoulder.* "SSSSSSSSSSSS, old woman!" said the old man. There is a plump quail sitting on your shoulder." He raised a broom handle * *and moved slowly forward. "Don't move!" he commanded. The old woman sat very still as the old man crept closer. Hunger was in their eyes.* * The old man swung a mighty blow with that broomstick, but Quail was too quick. * She flew up, and the broomstick bashed the old woman in the side of the head. * Her feet flew out, * up-ending the churn * and spilling the milk. * Her head jerked back, * hitting the wall and dislodging a bucket, * which came down to cover the old man's head. * "OLD FOOL!" she screamed, took the broomstick * *and began to beat the old man,* but * slipped in the milk and * fell flat on her back. The old man, blinded by the bucket, stepped forward, tripped on her * and * fell, pinning her to the ground. *The old man and old woman tussled and scolded for quite a spell before they sorted themselves out. Fox giggled, then laughed softly, then roared out loud.* It was a good joke, and he was mightily entertained.

As he stumbled away, still laughing, he heard another voice. It said, * "HICCUP!" Fox stopped. * "HICCUP!" "Who's there?" * "HICCUP!" "Who?" * "HICCUP!" said the hiccup. "I'm your hiccup." And, indeed, it was. * "HICCUP!" "How did you get here?" asked Fox. "You invited me. * HICCUP!" said the hiccup. "WELL, GO AWAY!" said Fox. "I can't * HICCUP! just go * HICCUP! away," said the hiccup. "You will have to help me go away." "How?" asked Fox. "Well, * HICCUP!" pondered the hiccup," * HICCUP! you could * HICCUP! put a paper * HICCUP! bag * HICCUP! over me, or hold * HICCUP! your breath, or * HICCUP! scare me away * HICCUP!"

*Off Fox * HICCUP! ran to Quail's tree. He * HICCUP! pounded on the trunk * HICCUP! of the tree. Quail heard the noise and her heart began to pound.* "Who's there?" she called down. * "HICCUP!" said the hiccup. "Me!" said Fox. * "HICCUP!" said the hiccup. "Fox!" said Fox. "What do you want?" asked Quail. "HELP!" cried Fox. * "HICCUP!" said the hiccup. "Come * HICCUP! down here * HICCUP! and find me something * HICCUP! to scare * HICCUP! away my hiccup, or...."

Quail flew down to sit next to Fox, but not too close. * "HICCUP!" said the hiccup. "Find me something to frighten away this * HICCUP! hiccup!" begged Fox. "Didn't I find you food when you were hungry, drink when you were thirsty, and entertainment when you wanted a good time? It should be enough," said Quail. "Please!" wailed Fox. * "HICCUP!" said the hiccup. "Very well," said Quail. But you must do exactly as I say! Close your eyes! Do not open them until I give the command! You will know how to follow because I will make a little humming noise with my wings. * Follow the noise. PROMISE!" "I promise," said Fox. * "HICCUP!" said the hiccup.

*Quail flew down the path, making a little humming noise with her wings. Fox * HICCUP! followed that noise, and though tempted * HIC-CUP to peek * HICCUP! he managed to * HICCUP! keep * HICCUP! his eyes * HICCUP! closed. Quail flew a long distance. At last, she came to the top of a hill.* There she found a hunter and his two dogs. The hunter was resting against a tree, holding his gun loosely. * "HICCUP!" said the hiccup. The dogs sat to attention, then pointed. The hunter saw a quail *flying low, followed by a fox with a hiccup. The fox's eyes appeared to be closed. Hunter and dogs didn't move. Quail led Fox directly up to the hunter,* then commanded that Fox open his eyes. * "HICCUP!" was the last thing the hiccup said before it departed, and then it was gone.

Fox was terrified. * *His ears laid flat, the hair on his back stood on end, his tail stiffened, his legs tensed, his claws dug into the ground, and his eyes, opened wide, fixed the hunter and dogs together in a frantic stare. Then he turned and ran. The dogs gave chase, baying as they came on. The hunter followed with his gun.*

Fox ran this way and that, out into the open and through brambles and bush. "Feet!" said Fox, "run for me." And his feet did. "Legs!" said Fox, "carry me." And his legs did. "Ears!" said Fox, "listen for me." And his ears did. "Eyes!" said Fox, "look out for me." And his eyes did. "Claws!" said Fox, "pull me along." And his claws did. But his tail became entangled in every bramble and snagged upon every branch.

Fox ran until he found a hole in a bank, the dogs right on his heels. He ducked into the hole, * sagged to the floor * and panted. * Then, he said, "Feet, what did you do to save me from the hunter?" *"We ran for you, Fox," they said.* "Legs," said Fox, "what did you do to save me from the hunter?" *"We carried you, Fox," they said.* "Ears," said Fox, "what did you do to save me from the hunter?" *"We listened for you, Fox," they said.* "Eyes," said Fox, "what did you do to save me from the hunter?" *"We watched out for you, Fox," they said.* "Claws," said Fox, "what did you do to save me from the hunter?" *"We pulled you along, Fox," they said.* "And tail," said Fox, "what did you do to save me from the hunter?" *"I caught on every bramble and branch to slow you down, Fox," it said.* Then, declared Fox, since you did not help me, tail, I shall give you to the hunter."

With that, Fox stuck his tail out of the hole. * The dogs and the hunter took hold of the tail * *and began to pull. "There!" said Fox to his tail. "The hunter shall have you. I cannot have baggage that does not help to save me." But, alas, the tail was attached to Fox, and as hunter and dogs pulled the tail, they pulled Fox with it. Fox dug and scratched and clawed to keep from being pulled out of the hole, but he could not hold on.* The hunter and the dogs had their way, Quail had her way, the hunter's wife decorated her best coat with fox fur her way—and it all happened because Fox had to have his way.

◀▶ ◀▶ ◀▶ ◀▶ ◀▶ ◀▶ ◀▶ ◀▶ ◀▶ ◀▶ ◀▶ ◀▶ ◀▶ ◀▶ ◀▶ ◀▶ ◀▶ ◀▶ ◀▶

All pot, pan, lid, and jar sound effects are storytellers' inventions which help to interpret the story. Experiment with pitch, intensity, and rhythm. Try similar inventions with other stories. "Mollie Whuppie" (Johnson et al. 1977), for example, contains a good amount of action, running, chasing, and general banging around. It might work nicely as a percussion story. And have a good time. It's all very theraputic.

Finger Plays

The Train

◄►◄►◄►◄►◄►◄►◄►◄►◄►◄►◄►◄►◄►◄►◄►◄►◄►

Finger plays contribute to a child's experience with story and language. They give each child opportunities to play with the rhythm and sounds of poetry, and reinforce sensory learning.

Finger plays can be grouped into several categories: nursery rhymes, occupations, sound play, holidays, parts of the body, and play. The following example uses sound play. Since almost every child is interested in trains, here is a finger play with a train story, sounds, and movements.

"Choo-choo-choo!"
[Slide hands together.]

The train runs down the track.
[Run fingers down arm.]

"Choo-choo-choo!"
[Slide hands together.]

And then it runs right back.
[Fingers run up arm.]

Here goes [child's name]'s train down the track.

"Choo-choo-choo-choo...."
[Slowly palm of hand slides down arm from shoulder to finger
    tips.]

Here comes [child's name]'s train up the track.

"Choo-choo-choo-choo!"
[Quickly palm of hand slides up the arm.]

(traditional)

◄►◄►◄►◄►◄►◄►◄►◄►◄►◄►◄►◄►◄►◄►◄►◄►◄►

The Steam Shovel

◀▶ ◀▶ ◀▶ ◀▶ ◀▶ ◀▶ ◀▶ ◀▶ ◀▶ ◀▶ ◀▶ ◀▶ ◀▶ ◀▶ ◀▶ ◀▶ ◀▶ ◀▶ ◀▶

Here in another finger play. Since children today see steam shovels in action at construction sites, this finger play will add to their concepts of the steam shovel. This example fits into the category of occupations.

If possible, visit a construction project and have the children watch a steam shovel in action.

Here is the steam shovel,
[Right forearm erect, hand drooping.]

And here is the ground.
[Two arms enclose area.]

See the great boom
[Right elbow stationary, forearm moving from side to side.]

Swing round and round.

It dips, it bites,
[Forearm dips, thumb and fingers in a grasping motion.]

It lifts, it throws.
[Forearm lifts, thumb and fingers spin.]

My, how the hole

In the ground grows!
[Two hands enclose circle.]

Dipping, scooping,

Lifting, throwing.

See how the hill
[Forearms with hands meeting.]

Beside it is growing.

(traditional)

◀▶ ◀▶ ◀▶ ◀▶ ◀▶ ◀▶ ◀▶ ◀▶ ◀▶ ◀▶ ◀▶ ◀▶ ◀▶ ◀▶ ◀▶ ◀▶ ◀▶ ◀▶ ◀▶

REFERENCES

Aardema, Verna. 1977. *Who's in Rabbit's House? A Masai Folktale*. New York: Dial.

_____. 1975. *Why Mosquitoes Buzz in People's Ears*. New York: Dial.

Aesop. 1968. *Aesop's Fables*. New York: Watts.

Alegria, Ricardo E. 1969. *Three Wishes: A Collection of Puerto Rican Folktales*. New York: Harcourt, Brace and World.

Arnott, Kathleen. 1971. *Animal Folktales around the World*. New York: Walck.

_____. 1963. *African Myths and Legends*. New York: Walck.

Asbjornsen, Peter Christian, and Jorgen Moe. 1960. *Norwegian Folk Tales*. New York: Viking.

Babbit, Ellen C. 1940. *Jataka Tales*. New York: Appleton-Century-Crofts.

Botkin, B. A. 1951. *A Treasury of Western Folklore*. New York: Crown.

_____. 1944. *A Treasury of American Folklore*. New York: Crown.

Bowman, James Cloyd, and Margery Bianco. 1964. *Tales from a Finnish Tupa*. Chicago: Albert Whitman.

Burton, William Frederick Padwick. 1962. *The Magic Drum: Tales from Central Africa*. New York: Criterion.

Carey, Bonnie. 1973. *Baba Yaga's Geese and Other Russian Stories*. Bloomington, Ind.: Indiana University Press.

Carrick, Valery J. 1970. *Still More Russian Picture Tales*. New York: Dover.

Cimino, Maria. 1970. *The Disobedient Eels and Other Italian Tales*. New York: Pantheon.

Colwell, Eileen. 1976. *The Magic Umbrella and Other Stories for Telling*. New York: McKay.

Courlander, Harold. 1970. *People of the Short Blue Corn: Tales and Legends of the Hopi Indians*. New York: Harcourt Brace Jovanovich.

_____. 1957. *Terrapin's Pot of Sense*. New York: Holt.

_____. 1947. *The Cow-Tail Switch and Other West African Stories*. New York: Holt, Rinehart and Winston.

Courlander, Harold, and Albert Kofi Prempeh. 1957. *The Hat-Shaking Dance and Other Tales from the Gold Coast*. New York: Harcourt Brace.

De La Mare, Walter. 1940. *Animal Stories*. New York: Scribner.

Diendorfer, Robert G. 1980. *America's 101 Most High Falutin', Big Talkin', Knee Slappin' Golly-whoppers and Tall Tales: The Best of the Burlington Liar's Club*. New York: Workman.

Dorliae, Peter G. 1970. *Animals Mourn for da Leopard and Other West African Tales*. Indianapolis, Ind.: Bobbs Merrill.

Frobenius, Leo, and Douglas C. Fox. 1966. *African Genesis*. New York: Benjamin Blom.

Gaer, Joseph. 1955. *The Fables of India*. Boston: Little, Brown.

Gilham, Charles E. 1943. *Beyond the Clapping Mountains: Eskimo Stories from Alaska*. New York: Macmillan.

Ginsburg, Mirra. 1973. *One Trick Too Many—Fox Stories from Russia*. New York: Dial.

_____. 1970. *The Three Rolls and One Doughtnut: Fables from Russia*. New York: Dial.

Green, Margaret. 1965. *The Big Book of Animal Fables*. New York: Watts.

Harrell, John. 1983. *The Man on a Dolphin*. Kensington, Calif.: York House.

Harris, John. 1986. American Folktales. *The Atlantic* 257 (April): 32-33.

Hatch, Mary Cottam. 1947. *Thirteen Danish Tales*. New York: Harcourt, Brace and World.

Hayes, Joe. 1982. *Coyote and....* Santa Fe, N. Mex.: Mariposa.

Heady, Eleanor B. 1965. *Jambo Sungura: Tales from East Africa*. New York: W. W. Norton.

Hitchcock, Patricia. 1966. *The King Who Rides a Tiger and Other Folk Tales from Nepal*. Berkeley, Calif.: Parnassus.

Hogrogian, Nonny. 1971. *One Fine Day*. New York: Macmillan.

Hume, Lotta Carswell. 1962. *Favorite Children's Stories from China and Tibet*. Rutland, Vt.: Charles E. Tuttle.

Jacobs, Joseph. 1892. *English Fairy Tales*. New York: Putnam.

Jagendorf, M. 1956. *The Priceless Cats and Other Italian Folk Stories*. New York: Vanguard.

Jagendorf, M. 1952. *Sand in the Bag and Other Folk Stories of Ohio, Indiana, and Illinois*. New York: Vanguard.

_____. 1950. *The Merry Men of Gotham*. New York: Vanguard.

_____. 1949a. *The Marvelous Adventures of Johnny Darling*. New York: Vanguard.

_____. 1949b. *Upstate Downstate: Folk Stories of the Middle Atlantic States*. New York: Vanguard.

_____. 1948. *New England Bean-Pot*. New York: Vanguard.

_____. 1938. *Tyll Ulenspiegel's Merry Pranks*. New York: Vanguard.

Jagendorf, Moritz A., and Ralph Steele Boggs. 1960. *The King of the Mountain: A Treasure of Latin American Folktales*. New York: Vanguard.

Johnson, Edna, et al. 1977. *Anthology of Children's Literature*. Boston: Houghton Mifflin.

Jones, Hettie. 1974. *Coyote Tales*. New York: Holt, Rinehart and Winston.

Jordan, Philip D. 1957. *Fiddlefoot Jones of the North Woods*. New York: Vanguard.

Knutson, Elnor. July, 1986. "Sudie and the Wagon Trains." Told at Eastern Montana College, Billings, Mont.

Korel, Edward, 1964. *Listen, and I'll Tell You*. Philadelphia, Pa.: Lippincott.

Lewis, Bobby. 1984. *Home before Midnight*. New York: Lothrop, Lee and Shepard.

Livo, Norma J., and Sandra A. Rietz. 1986. *Storytelling: Process and Practice*. Littleton, Colo.: Libraries Unlimited.

Maher, Ramona. 1969. *The Blind Boy and the Loon and Other Eskimo Myths*. New York: Day.

McDermott, Gerald. 1972. *Anansi the Spider: A Tale from the Ashanti*. New York: Holt, Rinehart and Winston.

Melzack, Ronald. 1970. *Raven, Creator of the World*. Boston: Little, Brown.

Montgomerie, Norah. 1961. *Twenty-Five Fables*. New York: Abelard-Schuman.

Pratt, Davis, and Elsa Kula. 1967. *Magic Animals of Japan*. Berkeley, Calif.: Parnassus.

Robinson, Gail, and Douglas Hill. 1976. *Coyote the Trickster: Legends of the North American Indians*. New York: Crane Russak.

Saltman, Judith. 1985. *The Riverside Anthology of Children's Literature*. Boston: Houghton Mifflin.

Schwartz, Alvin. 1975. *Whoppers, Tall Tales and Other Lies*. Philadelphia, Pa.: Lippincott.

Scofield, Elizabeth. 1965. *A Fox in One Bite and Other Tasty Tales from Japan*. Palo Alto, Calif.: Kodansha.

Sherlock, Philip M. 1966. *West Indian Folk Tales*. New York: Walck.

_____. 1954. *Anansi the Spider Man: Jamaican Folk Tales*. New York: Crowell.

Siddiqui, Ashraf, and Marilyn Lerch. 1961. *Toon-Toonie Pie and Other Tales from Pakistan*. Cleveland, Ohio: World.

Spellman, John. 1967. *The Beautiful Blue Jay and Other Tales of India*. Boston: Little, Brown.

Tashjian, Virginia A. 1966. *Once There Was and Was Not: Armenian Tales*. Boston: Little, Brown.

Tooze, Ruth, 1967. *Three Tales of Monkey: Ancient Folk Tales from the Far East*. New York: Day.

Wyatt, Isabel. 1962. *The Golden Stag and Other Folk Tales from India*. New York: McKay.

Zeitlin, Steven J., Amy J. Kotkin, and Holly Cutting Baker. 1982. *A Celebration of American Family Folklore: Tales and Traditions from the Smithsonian Collection*. New York: Pantheon.

5

Using Media in Storytelling

INTRODUCTION

Storytelling is itself a medium. It is a way of telling a story using the special devices of the live storyteller-audience interaction, the living oral language at its metaphoric best, and the characteristic paralinguistic effects which naturally attend the use of oral language. A storytelling is a special circumstance which is defined entirely by its context and by the literature which it operates. Its definition lies in its immediacy, its sponteniety, and its intimacy. Other means for telling stories exist, but only storytelling is storytelling.

Other media can be used to tell stories: dance, visual art, print, TV (video tape), computer software, radio (audio tape), music, and film. None of these is storytelling. If one of these other media is used to deliver a storytelling, then the problem of interferences between media surfaces. How can one medium be made to "carry" a second medium intact, such that the special, definitive characteristics of that second medium are not lost? A cursory consideration of the differences between the situation of the live storytelling and the limitations of each listed medium should serve to clarify the problem.

Perhaps some media—print, for instance—cannot portray a live storytelling at all. The other media might be considered as possibilities, provided that some careful calculations are made to minimize the loss of the effects of the live experience in the host medium. Radio, as an example, can be an effective extension of storytelling, if special attention is given to language and to those paralinguistic effects which can be heard, and if stories which are excessively visual are avoided. Television might also work. Here, special cautions must be observed that have to do with the habits of TV as they contradict the oral literature experience. For example, the primary interaction in a storytelling is that of audience and story through the medium of the storyteller. Camera shifts away from the storyteller show the viewing audience the reactions of the studio audience. This takes the viewing audience out of the story itself and makes them spectators. Camera shots of pictures intended to illustrate the story violate the mental imagery principle, which is at the foundation of the storytelling act. Other media will present restrictions of their own, imposing these restrictions upon a storytelling and limiting its definition.

Some suggestions for combining storytelling with selected other media are given here. Individuals who wish to use another medium to "carry" or to otherwise portray storytelling and the storytelling experience, must carefully consider the specifics of each case.

RADIO STORYTELLINGS

Consider taking stories before the public on radio. Public radio stations often do local programming, and storytelling is usually a welcome addition to the scope of programming available. Storytelling reaches a greater audience, in terms of interest, than do many programs, and provides fare for younger listeners. There are several ways to approach radio stations:

1. Make a tape. Present it in person to the program director. Talk about storytelling, identifying its general interest and its audience. You may have to teach and tell at the same time. Specify a time for checking back.

2. Contact the program director about programming for fund raising. The fund-raising week quite often includes local performers. Volunteer.

3. Offer to come into the studio to make a tape for use by the station. The programming people will have a chance to see you work and to get a feeling for both the application of storytelling to radio and the power of storytelling in general.

4. If you happen to teach a storytelling class, persuade the program director to allow select students (perhaps as a requirement for graduate credit) to make a tape of one story each under studio conditions. Promise to review the material along with the program director, and to help make selections and cuts. Offer to sit in when (if) the tapes are played over the air to provide background and commentary.

Studio tapings are lonesome experiences for a storyteller. Most tellers are used to an audience. The audience "feeds" the story and the telling. And since the audience is, in fact, a part of the story, working without an audience is like working without a part of the story. You might volunteer to do a live telling for a fund-raising event, scheduling the telling for an early evening, when families of station employees are present—a ready audience. Otherwise, the audience will be the microphone and the sound engineer.

If this last circumstance is the case, remember that the audience is displaced. The immediacy of the physical story, the context embeddedness of the story is changed considerably for the audience. The manner in which the story is told will be dependent upon the situation—microphone and sound engineer. The story will have to be tailored somewhat to accommodate the fact that visual effects cannot be seen. All story imagery will depend upon the successful employment of the many devices of sound. Run the story through several times before making an appearance at the station. Such efforts will insure radio-appropriate effects.

MURALS

Historically, there are many examples of artistic expression accompanying the telling of a story. Many art forms such as the Javanese shadow puppets, the storyboards of Palau, and the storytelling tapestries of India are an integral component of an oral tradition.

Drawing pictures of scenes from a familiar story not only demonstrates comprehension but also artistically extends the storytelling experience. We have many accessible forms of technology available to do this. The following idea involves using 35mm slides, but 16mm moving pictures and video tape could also be used.

Ask a group or an individual to create a mural of scenes from a story just heard. Photograph these mural scenes with 35mm slide film. The slides could then accompany the story in a multi-media presentation either with a live storyteller or an audio tape of the storyteller. Share this production with others.

TELEVISION

With the current ease of videotaping and playback, a whole new area of technology is available for use in storytelling. The fact that a live storyteller is superior to any performance as seen on television cannot really be argued. The live storyteller is a powerful being. But should we disregard television entirely? Are there any legitimate uses for it in conjunction with storytelling?

Television is being used presently in several ways. Jay O'Callahan has developed a 33-minute tape (it also is available in 16mm movie format), *A Master Class in Storytelling* (1983. Vineyard Video Productions, Elias Lane, West Tisbury, MA 02575). On this tape Jay is seated in a library and is being interviewed. He discusses why we tell stories, how to tell stories, and the uses of storytelling as a teaching activity or an art form. This tape was awarded first prize for teacher education at the 1985 National Educational Film Festival. Obviously, this tape has already received acceptance among educators.

The tape of a performance also can be used to evaluate style and technique. The recording and playback ease of an actual telling can be valuable to the storyteller for self-evaluation as well as critical analysis.

Several graduate students at the University of Colorado at Denver, using an interview format, videotaped Colorado storytellers. Their purpose was to ask each teller why he or she felt that storytelling was important. Then the discussion became more informal. Their project made it possible via the tape to bring six storytellers into an already crowded classroom. It also provided material for class discussion about storytelling, styles, and values.

Certainly a video library of storytellings could also be used by organizations interested in obtaining the services of a professional storyteller. They could easily base their decisions on taped performances rather than on word-of-mouth impressions of others.

The efforts of storytellers on commercial television could be viewed and evaluated. We are seeing the performances of more syndicated storytellers as well as local storytellers on cable channels. Did the use of special effects add anything to the telling? Did their use detract?

There are many more ideas involving the use of television and storytelling. Have a group brainstorm some of these uses. How could television be used with storytelling to help promote it? How can storytellers capitalize on the technology that is available?

After such a brainstorming session, people might be motivated to experiment with television. It will be interesting to see what kinds of collaborations there will be between television and storytellers in the future.

6

Thinking It Over

INTRODUCTION

The activities in this chapter provide a variety of "thinking it over" ideas. All of the suggestions are quite functional. How does a prospective storyteller get started? In this chapter there is a list of tips that may answer that question.

There are also games and activities that fit the mood of the chapter. The word games and puzzles are not only amusing in themselves but can also serve the function of review and assimilation. The "Cooperative Learning" activity, for example, could encourage a multi-age school experience in which all participants would benefit personally. Other projects call attention to ongoing storytelling activities. Altogether, chapter 6 is one of reflection and analysis.

TIPS FOR STORYTELLING

The first thing most people ask when it looks as if they are going to become involved in actually telling a story, is "How do you do it?" There are absolutely no hard and fast rules. Everything (except the first point enumerated below) is subject to individual preferences. Whatever works for you is right. Whatever you feel comfortable doing is right for you. These ideas are suggestions that you might want to consider.

1. Choose a story you are familiar with and like.

2. If it is a story from printed sources, read it two or three times.

3. Get the main order of the story in your mind. What are the important points? What is the sequence of events?

4. Try telling the story to yourself.

5. Reread the story.

6. Add the parts you have left out. Do not memorize, except for specific rhymes.

7. Try telling the story in front of a mirror. This works for some and not for others.

8. If you have a tape recorder, tape the story and listen to it critically.

9. Videotape yourself telling the story. Evaluate it critically.

10. Tell the story again in front of a mirror or for your family, friends, or groups of children.

11. Add facial and hand expressions and any noises or sounds that fit.

12. Keep your eyes moving over the people to whom you are telling the story; sit or stand close to your audience.

13. Use pauses wisely. Don't be afraid of them.

14. Use your voice for character traits and to express suspense, surprise, joy, sorrow, quietness, etc.

15. Write down specific rhymes or the beginning and ending on cards if you think you might need them as a reminder just before you start the story.

16. Can you add any poetry, songs, or folklore to your story?

17. What can you add to the story to make it yours? Sometimes we get flashes of inspiration while actually telling the story. Make a note of these inspirations.

18. Practice.

19. Good luck telling your stories.

SHORT GAMES AND ACTIVITIES

Folklore Dictionary

◄►◄►◄►◄►◄►◄►◄►◄►◄►◄►◄►◄►◄►◄►◄►◄►◄►◄►

Place the following words in alphabetical order and write a definition for each one. If you need help, refer to a dictionary.

tradition	folklore
minstrel	anthropologist
culture	legend
heroine	yarn
tall tales	troubadour
bard	folklorist
epic	mythology
fairy tale	hero
fable	proverb

Keep your dictionary either in the storytelling journal you started or make and illustrate a separate folklore dictionary. These storytelling vocabulary exercises will be useful in telling stories or writing reports.

◄►◄►◄►◄►◄►◄►◄►◄►◄►◄►◄►◄►◄►◄►◄►◄►◄►◄►

Folk Tale Puzzle

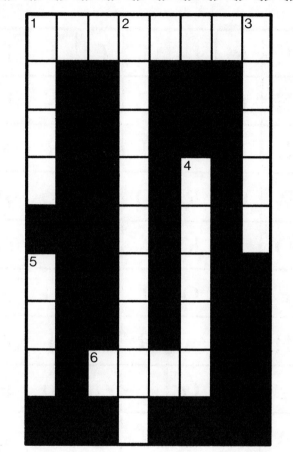

ACROSS

1. Cinderella lost one of her glass _____.

6. The prince woke Sleeping Beauty with a _____.

DOWN

1. The Ugly Duckling became a beautiful _____.

2. A wooden puppet who turned into a boy. _____.

3. Snow White lived with _____ dwarfs.

4. Goldilocks visited the three _____.

5. A little _____ helped make shoes for the shoemaker.

Word Search

◄►◄►◄►◄►◄►◄►◄►◄►◄►◄►◄►◄►◄►◄►◄►◄►

C	E	R	U	T	C	I	P	O
B	H	C	S	C	E	N	E	F
J	L	A	S	T	O	R	Y	G
M	W	O	R	D	S	K	P	H
F	O	L	K	A	O	S	G	T
V	P	L	O	T	C	U	Z	W
C	H	E	A	R	A	T	A	F
H	E	T	G	L	I	D	E	X
B	A	N	E	T	S	I	L	R

Find the following words and circle them. They may be horizontal, vertical, backwards, or diagonal.

hear	story	tell	picture
words	plot	laugh	character
scene	folk	listen	

◄►◄►◄►◄►◄►◄►◄►◄►◄►◄►◄►◄►◄►◄►◄►◄►

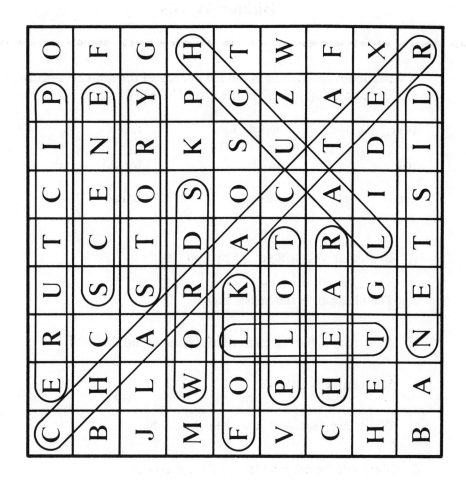

Answers to pages 111 and 112.

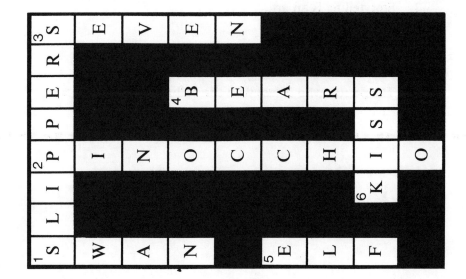

Hidden Words

◀▶ ◀▶ ◀▶ ◀▶ ◀▶ ◀▶ ◀▶ ◀▶ ◀▶ ◀▶ ◀▶ ◀▶ ◀▶ ◀▶ ◀▶ ◀▶ ◀▶ ◀▶

A word about storytelling is hidden in each of the sentences below. The first one is marked for you. Find the rest. The words are:

hear	word	listen
tell	myth	legend
sing	story	ballad

1. Be fast or you will get hit by that car.

2. The blue ball is ten inches high.

3. Your foot is the leg end and the hand is the arm end.

4. My thimble is golden.

5. Which did Jack get? A sow or donkey?

6. Mary and he are next in line for ice cream.

7. Storytelling is an art.

8. He without sin gets the halo.

9. The person who is last with the ball advances two spaces.

◀▶ ◀▶ ◀▶ ◀▶ ◀▶ ◀▶ ◀▶ ◀▶ ◀▶ ◀▶ ◀▶ ◀▶ ◀▶ ◀▶ ◀▶ ◀▶ ◀▶ ◀▶

Answers to page 114.

1. Be fa|st or y|ou will get hit by that car.

2. The blue bal|l is ten| inches high.

3. Your foot is the |leg end| and the hand is the arm end.

4. |My th|imble is golden.

5. Which did Jack get? A so|w or d|onkey?

6. Mary and |he ar|e next in line for ice cream.

7. Story|tell|ing is an art.

8. He without |sin g|ets the halo.

9. The person who is last with the |ball ad|vances two spaces.

Traveling Story

◄►◄►◄►◄►◄►◄►◄►◄►◄►◄►◄►◄►◄►◄►◄►◄►◄►◄►◄►

Have everyone sit in a circle. Whisper into the first person's ear, "Fifty cups of Crisco makes a great big fluffy fritter." Each one, in turn, whispers the message to the next person. The last person to hear the phrase tells everyone what it was that he or she heard.

Did the phrase change much in the telling? If so, how? Find out what caused any changes.

◄►◄►◄►◄►◄►◄►◄►◄►◄►◄►◄►◄►◄►◄►◄►◄►◄►◄►◄►

Cooperative Learning

High school students can learn better storytelling and story writing skills by working with primary grade students. Match each high schooler with a primary school child. For the first session, have each high school student select and prepare a story to tell to the primary student partner. Try it out with the youngster. Encourage the pair to discuss what they liked about the story and what made the storytelling work. Why did the high school student choose that story to tell?

In the next session, have each primary school child dictate a story to the older partner. The high school partner will then type the story and illustrate it for the younger child.

In the third session, the pair will share the dictated story and the pictures. The younger child will get this project as a gift.

For the fourth session, have the high school student examine what makes a good story. What makes a story work? Then each of the high school students will write an original story, and reproduce it on pages leaving ample space for illustrations. During this fourth session, the older students will tell and read their stories and leave the texts for the primary children to illustrate later.

At the fifth and final session, the pairs can share the added art. The primary children will tell the stories to their partners. Together they can then discuss telling, writing, and illustrating stories. In these five sessions both individuals in each of the pairs will have learned a lot together.

The language arts skills utilized by each student include reading, writing, listening, and speaking, along with a variety of problem-solving, artistic, and creative skills. All of the students involved will actually work not only on academic learning but also on interpersonal skills.

In family living classes, these experiences will provide skills useful immediately in baby sitting as well as establish a model for the future when these high school students assume the responsibilities of parenthood.

To extend their relationship and their experiences, the students might plan to write a poem or song to go with one of the stories.

Bulletin Boards

Develop a bulletin board to celebrate storytelling. This board could be used as the backdrop for storytelling sessions.

Here are some ideas:

1. Use the theme of a prospector panning for gold. Have the listeners write the titles of stories they have told on round pieces of gold paper and place them like gold nuggets in the stream.

2. Use the theme of "tall tales." Have each person find local tall tales, practice telling them, illustrate them, and add them to the bulletin board.

If there is no bulletin board available where the storytelling sessions are held, you might want to use for your displays the walls of the gymnasium, rooms, or hallways where storytelling takes place.

REVIEW PROJECTS

The Origins of Stories

◄►◄►◄►◄►◄►◄►◄►◄►◄►◄►◄►◄►◄►◄►◄►◄►◄►◄►

There are many stories that explain how stories came to be. Research some of these tales. For example, how did Anansi get stories? What do Native Americans tell us about where stories came from?

List all of the information and the titles and references you find. Add to this list as you find more explanations.

If possible, have a group share all of the different origins they found. Next, each person could tell or write their own version of the origin of stories.

◄►◄►◄►◄►◄►◄►◄►◄►◄►◄►◄►◄►◄►◄►◄►◄►◄►◄►

Telling a Story

◄►◄►◄►◄►◄►◄►◄►◄►◄►◄►◄►◄►◄►◄►◄►◄►◄►◄►

After reading some different author's ideas about how to tell a story, list 25 steps for telling a story. What are some of the techniques and processes that effective storytellers use?

Mark Twain wrote a humorous essay on "How to Tell a Story" (in Botkin 1983, 499-500). Read his remarks after making your list. He adds another point of view to telling stories.

◄►◄►◄►◄►◄►◄►◄►◄►◄►◄►◄►◄►◄►◄►◄►◄►◄►◄►

Prairie Home Companion

Objective: To develop the ability to analyze a storyteller's style.

Garrison Keillor, the creator and star of the radio series "A Prairie Home Companion," which can be heard weekly on public radio stations, created and populated Lake Wobegon. Thousands of faithful listeners enjoy his stories, some of which have been collected in a book (Keillor 1985) and on tapes (1985, 1983). Since imitation is the sincerest form of flattery, can you invent and create stories with your own place and people?

Analyze Garrison Keillor's stories for their flavor, content, detail, and style. This would make a rich group activity in which people could study Keillor's stories and discuss them. What made the stories work? How did Keillor make the stories appeal to listeners?

REFERENCES

Botkin, B. A., ed. 1983. *A Treasury of American Folklore*. New York: Bonanza Books.

Keillor, Garrison. 1985. *Lake Wobegon Days*. New York: Viking.

_____. *Gospel Birds and Other Stories of Lake Wobegon*. 1985. St. Paul, Minn.: Minnesota Public Radio. Cassette tape.

_____. *News from Lake Wobegon*. 1983. St. Paul, Minn.: Minnesota Public Radio. Cassette tapes.

Appendices

A

Evaluating Storytelling

Throughout these activities, folks are being called on to actually tell stories. If possible, videotape a storyteller telling a story and have the participants evaluate the teller and discuss their observations. It would be preferable to view the tape once for enjoyment and then a second time for the evaluation.

Have the viewers develop a checklist for their evaluations. If essential items are omitted from the original list, add them yourself. A good checklist might read as follows.

The storyteller was (1) able to, (2) sometimes able to, (3) not able to:

	(1)	(2)	(3)
motivate the audience to listen	___	___	___
convey action vividly	___	___	___
convey sequence of events clearly	___	___	___
assume character's point of view	___	___	___
express human motives	___	___	___

	(1)	(2)	(3)
express human conflict	_____	_____	_____
express human values	_____	_____	_____
establish mood	_____	_____	_____
use figurative language	_____	_____	_____
use language rhythmically	_____	_____	_____
speak clearly and distinctly	_____	_____	_____
utilize varied intonation	_____	_____	_____
utilize appropriate gestures	_____	_____	_____
utilize eye contact effectively	_____	_____	_____
end the story gracefully	_____	_____	_____

B

Storytelling Journal

Start a storytelling journal to document your storytelling activities. Include programs, announcements, and other material on storytelling concerts, swaps, and conferences you attend. Look for storytelling events held at local schools, libraries, museums, or folklore societies. You may want to travel to areas which conduct regular festivals such as Jonesborough, Tennessee during the first weekend of October each year for the National Association for the Preservation and Perpetuation of Storytelling festival.

What were the sources for the stories you heard? Ask the storytellers if you are not sure whether the story was from folklore, modern literature, or the teller's imagination.

YOUR TELLINGS

Put copies of any stories you tell, pictures of you telling stories, and any news items printed about your presentations into your journal. If there are no news clippings, write up your own.

Keep notes for yourself about how the sessions went, new story ideas that came to you, and any storytelling insights you had. It might help in the future if you have a record of that great line that came to you when you were in the middle of telling a story. Sometimes we get flashes of insight and invent wondrous variations while in action. Sometimes the story reveals itself to us while we are telling it.

CONTENTS

This journal could serve as a progress report for your storytelling activities. It can remind you of things that worked, or did not work, and document your development as a storyteller.

It is also conceivable that you may refer to this journal as you develop a resume for use in professional engagements. Since most organizations want to know where you have told stories, for whom, and what kinds of stories you tell, the journal can become an information resource and reminder.

You could also keep a copy of family stories that could be developed into some everyday storytelling situation. Another suggestion is to include notes on ideas for creating original stories.

FORMAT

A loose-leaf photograph album with sticky sides on the pages and plastic overlays makes a convenient journal format. Such an album also protects newspaper articles, which tend to get crumbly. This format also is flexible and allows you to insert and rearrange the pages. Whatever format you choose for your journal, the important thing is to start your journal now.

C

Matrix of Skills and Activities

The following matrix includes several pieces of information for each storytelling activity. First, different kinds of activities are matched with the kinds of educational skills they utilize; second, the activities are identified with a level of Bloom's taxonomy; next they are categorized by type (e.g., listening, writing) and whether they are group or individual activities; then they are identified according to appropriate ages of participants; and finally they are listed by page number in the text.

EDUCATIONAL SKILLS*

1. realize the importance of literature as a mirror of human experiences, reflecting human motives, conflicts, and values

2. be able to identify with fictional characters in human situations as a means of relating to others; gain insights from involvement with literature

3. become aware of important writers representing diverse backgrounds and traditions in literature.

---

*From *Essentials of English*. National Council of Teachers of English. 1982. Urbana, Illinois: NCTE.

4. become familiar with masterpieces of literature, both past and present

5. develop effective ways of talking and writing about varied forms of literature

6. experience literature as a way to appreciate the rhythms and beauty of language

7. develop habits of reading that carry over into adult life

8. to speak clearly and expressively about ideas and concerns

9. to adapt words and strategies according to varying situations and audiences, from one-to-one conversations to formal, large-group settings

10. to participate productively and harmoniously in both small and large groups

11. to present arguments in orderly and convincing ways

12. to interpret and access various kinds of communication, including intonation, pause, gesture, and body language, that accompany speaking

13. learn that listening with understanding depends on determining a speaker's purpose

14. learn to attend to detail and relate it to the over-all purpose of the communication

15. learn to evaluate the messages and effects of mass communication

16. recognize that reading functions as a pleasurable activity as well as a means of acquiring knowledge

17. learn from the very beginning to approach reading as a search for meaning

18. develop the necessary reading skills to comprehend material appearing in a variety of forms

19. learn to read accurately and make valid inferences

20. learn to judge literature critically on the basis of personal response and literary quality

21. learn to write clearly and honestly

22. recognize that writing is a way to learn and develop personally as well as a way to communicate with others

23. learn to adapt expression to various audiences

24. learn the techniques of writing from appealing to others and persuading them

25. develop talents for creative and imaginative expression

26. recognize that precision in punctuation, capitalization, spelling, and other elements of manuscript form is a part of the total effectiveness of writing

27. learn that originality derives from the uniqueness of the individual's perception, not necessarily from an innate talent

28. learn that inventiveness involves seeing new relationships

29. learn that creative thinking derives from the ability not only to look, but to see; not only to hear, but to listen; not only to imitate, but to innovate; not only to observe, but to experience the excitement of fresh perception

30. learn to create hypotheses and predict outcomes

31. learn to understand logical relationships

32. learn to construct logical sequences and understand the conclusions to which they lead

33. to detect fallacies in reasoning

34. to recognize that "how to think" is different from "what to think"

35. to ask questions in order to discover meaning

36. to differentiate between subjective and objective viewpoints; to discriminate between opinion and fact

37. to evaluate the intentions and messages of speakers and writers, especially attempts to manipulate the language in order to deceive

38. to make judgments based on criteria that can be supported and explained

BLOOM'S TAXONOMY LEVELS*

K = Knowledge

Indicators of the knowledge level would be the words *cite, collect, define, enumerate, know, label, list, memorize, name, recall, record, recount, relate, repeat, specify,* and *tell.*

C = Comprehension

Indicators of the comprehension level would be the words *describe, discuss, explain, express, identify, locate, recognize, report, restate, retell, review, summarize,* and *translate.*

Ap = Application

Indicators of the application level would be the words *apply, calculate, demonstrate, dramatize, employ, exhibit, experiment, illustrate, interview, operate, practice, show, simulate, solve,* and *use.*

An = Analysis

Indicators of the analysis level would be the words *analyze, arrange, categorize, classify, compare, contrast, detect, diagram, differentiate, discover, dissect, distinguish, examine, group, inquire, inspect, interpret, inventory, investigate, organize, probe, question, scrutinize, survey,* and *test.*

S = Synthesis

Indicators of the synthesis level would be the words *arrange, assemble, compose, concoct, construct, contrive, create, design, develop, formulate, generalize, hypothesize, imagine, incorporate, invent, originate, plan, predict, prepare, produce, propose, set up,* and *systematize.*

E = Evaluation

Indicators of the evaluation level would be the words *appraise, assess, choose, compare, conclude, criticize, decide, deduce, determine, estimate, evaluate, infer, judge, measure, predict, rate, recommend, revise, score, select,* and *value.*

---

*Adapted from Benjamin S. Bloom, et al. 1956. *Taxonomy of Educational Objectives: Handbook I: Cognitive Domain.* New York: David McKay.

Category

Storytelling activities in this book can be used either by individuals or groups. They also fall into the following categories, with some activities fitting into several categories.

1. All purpose activity

2. Entertainment activity

3. Literary activity

4. Listening activity

5. Social activity

6. Speaking activity

7. Reading activity

8. Writing activity

9. Art or music activity

Level

This designation refers to approximate educational level of the participants.

1. Preschool

2. Elementary

3. Secondary

4. All ages

Matrix

Storytelling Activity	Educational Skill	Bloom's Taxonomy Level	Category	Group Activity	Individual Activity	Level	Page
ADDING MUSIC TO A STORY	6, 14, 28, 29, 30, 31	S	4, 6, 7, 9		X	2, 3, 4	32
AMERICAN REGIONAL STORIES	1, 2, 7, 16, 17	S, E	3, 7		X	3	78
AND THEN WHAT HAPPENED	10, 14, 28, 30, 32	S, E	1, 2, 4, 5, 6	X		4	6
BOOKS ABOUT STORYTELLING	5, 17, 18, 19, 21, 28, 30, 31, 32 35	E	7, 8		X	2, 3, 4	139
BROWN BEAR, BROWN BEAR, WHAT DO YOU SEE?	6, 16, 19, 21, 22	K, C	3, 4, 6, 8, 9		X	1, 2	10
BULLETIN BOARDS	27, 28	Ap, S	2, 5	X	X	4	116
CIRCLE SWAP OF PERSONAL HISTORY OR EXPERIENCE	8, 10, 12, 14, 27, 28, 29, 32	S	1, 2, 4, 5, 6	X		1, 2, 3, 4	86
CONTROLLING THE ELEMENTS OF DELIVERY – PRACTICE	8, 9, 12 27, 29, 37	An	1		X	4	52
COOPERATIVE LEARNING	1, 4, 5, 6, 7, 8, 9, 10, 12, 14, 17, 19, 20, 21, 22	E	1, 2, 3	X		3, 4, 5, 6, 7, 8	116
CRAZY CRITTERS	10, 12, 28, 38	C	1	X	X	4	8

Matrix (*continued*)

Storytelling Activity	Educational Skill	Bloom's Taxonomy Level	Category	Group Activity	Individual Activity	Level	Page
CREATING VISUAL IMAGERY	5, 6, 10 14, 15, 17, 19, 32	E	3, 4, 5, 7	X		4	53
DOLPHINS	1, 4, 5, 8, 11, 16, 18, 20, 21, 22, 25, 27	E	3, 6, 7, 8		X	2, 3, 4	2
FAMILY FOLKLORE	22, 25, 26, 29	S	1		X	2, 3	69
FOLKLORE DICTIONARY	17	K	7		X	2, 3	110
FOLK TALE PUZZLE	4, 18, 19	C	3, 7		X	2	111
FROGERATURE	25, 27, 30	S	1		X	2, 3, 4	11
GAMES AND DANCES	12, 27, 28, 29	Ap	1	X		4	57
GROUP STORY DEVELOPMENT	9, 10, 12, 13, 14, 28, 32, 37	S	1	X		4	51
GUIDED FANTASY	13, 14, 15, 27, 34	Ap	1, 2	X		4	14
HEARING MAGIC	15, 25, 27, 28, 29	E	1, 4, 6, 8		X	2, 3, 4	62

(Matrix continues on page 132.)

Matrix (*continued*)

Storytelling Activity	Educational Skill	Bloom's Taxonomy Level	Category	Group Activity	Individual Activity	Level	Page
HERE IS A GOOD ONE FOR YOU	9, 10, 13, 14, 27, 28, 29	S	1, 4 5, 6	X		2, 3, 4	6
HEROES AND HEROINES	8, 9, 10, 11 12, 14, 27, 28, 29, 32	E	1, 4, 5, 6	X		2, 3, 4	4
HIDDEN WORDS	16, 17, 18, 19, 28	Ap	7		X	4	114
THE HOUSEWIFE'S LAMENT	1, 2, 5, 6, 11, 14, 21, 22, 25, 27, 28, 29	E	1, 3, 4, 8, 9	X	X		42
HOW DID THAT STORY GO?	1, 2, 4, 7, 10, 12, 14, 17, 18, 20, 32	S	1	X		4	21
JACK TALES	27, 28, 29, 30, 31, 32	E	1, 5	X		2, 3, 4	62
LITERARY STORIES	16, 17, 18, 19, 20	An	7		X	3,4	3
MAGIC HAT	8, 9, 10 11, 14, 27, 28, 29	E	1, 4, 5, 6	X		2, 3, 4	14
MAKING A BALLAD	4, 5, 6, 14, 23, 25, 27, 28	E	1, 3, 4, 6, 8, 9	X	X	2, 3, 4	38

Matrix (*continued*)

Storytelling Activity	Educational Skill	Bloom's Taxonomy Level	Category	Group Activity	Individual Activity	Level	Page
MEMORIES	10, 11, 12, 14, 27, 28, 29, 32	E	1, 4, 5, 6	X		2, 3, 4	88
MIRROR, MIRROR ON THE WALL	8, 10, 27, 28, 29	S	1, 2, 4, 5, 6	X		1, 2, 3, 4	5
MONITORING PRE-TELLING PROTOCOLS	12, 28, 29	E	1		X	4	48
MORE DOLPHINS	1, 4, 5, 7, 17, 18, 27, 28, 29, 32	S	1, 3, 7, 8		X	2, 3, 4	65
MOVING POSTURES	12, 27, 28, 29, 30	Ap	1, 5	X		4	60
MURALS	13, 14, 27, 28, 29	S 5	1, 4, 3, 4	X		1, 2,	106
MY MOST EMBARRASSING MOMENT	8, 9, 10, 11 12, 14, 27, 28, 29, 32	E	1, 4, 6	X		2, 3, 4	89
MYTHS	4, 5, 7, 16, 17, 18, 19, 22, 25, 27, 28, 29, 32	E	1, 3, 7, 8		X	2, 3, 4	68
NEWSPAPER STORIES	1, 2, 5, 7, 21, 22, 24, 25, 27, 28	E	1, 3, 7, 8		X	2, 3, 4	2

(Matrix continues on page 134.)

Matrix (*continued*)

Storytelling Activity	Educational Skill	Bloom's Taxonomy Level	Category	Group Activity	Individual Activity	Level	Page
NO SUCH THINGS	3, 10, 14, 25, 27, 28, 29	E 6, 8	1, 2, 4,	X		2, 3, 4	9
NURSERY RHYMES	4, 6, 10, 14, 27, 28, 29	An, S	4, 5, 6	X		1, 2	82
OCCUPATIONS IN FOLKTALES	1, 3, 4, 5, 9, 17, 27, 28	E	1		X	4	4
THE OLD WOMAN AND HER PIG	4, 5, 6, 10, 14, 17, 20, 28	An	1, 2, 3, 4, 5, 6, 8	X		1, 2, 3, 4	76
THE ORIGINS OF STORIES	1, 4, 7, 17, 18, 19, 22, 25, 27, 28, 29, 32	E	3, 7, 8		X	2, 3, 4	117
PARTICIPATION STORIES	4, 5, 6, 10, 25, 30	E	3, 5, 6, 7		X	2, 3	90
PASS THE STORY	27, 28, 29, 30, 31, 32	S	1, 2, 4, 6	X		2, 3, 4	6
PERCUSSION STORIES	2, 4, 14, 30, 35	S	1	X		4	93
PERFORMING FAMILY HISTORY	9, 10, 11, 12, 27, 28, 29, 32	E	1, 2, 4, 6	X	X	2, 3, 4	84

Matrix (*continued*)

Storytelling Activity	Educational Skill	Bloom's Taxonomy Level	Category	Group Activity	Individual Activity	Level	Page
PICK AN OBJECT, PICK ANY OBJECT	9, 10, 11, 13, 14, 27, 28, 29, 35	An	1	X		4	11
PLAYING SCHEHERAZADE	4, 5, 9, 10, 11, 14, 27, 28, 29, 32	E	1, 3, 4, 5, 6	X		2, 3, 4	8
POINT OF VIEW	5, 9, 10, 14, 27, 28, 29, 32	E	1, 4, 5, 6	X		2, 3, 4	32
POSTURED TELLING	12, 27, 28, 29	Ap	1	X		4	58
PRAIRIE HOME COMPANION	12, 13, 14, 15, 21, 22, 25, 27, 28, 29, 36	An	1, 4, 5, 6, 8	X	X	2, 3, 4	117
RADIO STORYTELLINGS	8, 9, 11, 29, 32, 37	E	1, 2, 6, 8		X	2, 3, 4	105
RAINBOW STORIES	1, 4, 7, 25, 27, 28, 29, 31, 32	E	3, 7, 8		X	2, 3, 4	69
RITUAL OBJECTS	28, 29	E	1		X	4	50
RITUAL OPENINGS AND CLOSINGS	25, 27	E	1		X	4	46

(Matrix continues on page 136.)

Matrix (*continued*)

Storytelling Activity	Educational Skill	Bloom's Taxonomy Level	Category	Group Activity	Individual Activity	Level	Page
SIGN LANGUAGE	10, 12, 18	S	1, 5		X	2, 3, 4	62
SPONTANEOUS CREATIVITY	9, 10, 12, 14, 27, 28, 29, 32	S	1, 4, 5, 6	X		2, 3, 4	4
THE STEAM SHOVEL	14, 28, 29, 30, 33	Ap	1, 4, 5	X		1, 2	99
STORY-INITIATING QUOTATIONS	1, 4, 6, 7	E	1		X	4	46
STORY MAPPING – AFTER THE TELLING	5, 14, 28, 30, 31, 32, 35, 38	E	1	X		4	17
STORY MAPPING – BEFORE THE TELLING	5, 10, 14, 22, 28, 30	E	1	X		4	25
STORY MAPPING – TO CREATE A STORY	14, 22, 25, 28, 30, 35	E	1	X		4	12
THE STORYTELLER	1, 2, 4, 7, 17, 18, 19, 22, 27, 28, 29, 32	E	3, 4, 6, 7, 8		X	2, 3, 4	74
STORYTELLING JOURNAL	21, 22, 24, 25, 27, 28, 29, 30, 32	E	1, 8		X	2, 3 4	123

Matrix (*continued*)

Storytelling Activity	Educational Skill	Bloom's Taxonomy Level	Category	Group Activity	Individual Activity	Level	Page
STORYTELLING WARM-UP IDEAS	8, 9, 12, 27, 28, 29, 31, 32, 35, 37	all levels	1, 4, 5, 6	X		4	7
STRETCHING	12, 29	Ap	1	X		4	55
STRINGING STORIES TOGETHER	6, 19, 28, 29, 30, 32, 35, 38	E	1		X	4	80
TAILORING A STORY— PARTICIPATION	14, 29, 30, 31, 32, 35	E	1, 4	X		4	90
TAILORING A STORY— STRUCTURE	4, 5, 6, 7, 28, 29, 31, 38	7	1		X	4	28
TELEVISION	8, 10, 11, 15, 28, 29, 38	A, An, S, E	1	X		4	106
TELLING A STORY	17, 18, 19, 22, 26, 31, 32, 35, 38	C	1, 7		X	4	117
THE TRAIN	14, 28, 29, 30, 33	Ap	1, 4, 5	X		1, 2	98
TIPS FOR STORYTELLING	12, 13, 14, 20, 25	An, S, E	1		X	4	108

(Matrix continues on page 138.)

Matrix (*continued*)

Storytelling Activity	Educational Skill	Bloom's Taxonomy Level	Category	Group Activity	Individual Activity	Level	Page
TRAVELING STORY	10, 14, 32	E	1, 2, 4, 5, 6	X 3, 4		1, 2,	115
A TRICKSTER SWAP	1, 2, 4, 9, 10, 12, 14, 17, 18, 19, 27, 28, 29, 32	E	1, 3, 4, 5, 6, 7	X		2, 3, 4	70
VARIATIONS ON A THEME	27, 28, 29, 30, 31, 32, 34, 35	E	3, 7, 8		X	2, 3, 4	78
VARIANTS	4, 5, 6, 27, 28, 29, 30, 31, 32, 33, 34	E	3, 6, 7, 8		X	2, 3, 4	78
WORD SEARCH	17, 18, 19, 30, 31, 32	K	1, 7		X	2, 3, 4	112
YESTERDAY	8, 9, 10, 11, 12, 14, 27, 28, 29, 32	E	1, 4, 5, 6, 8	X		2, 3, 4	89

D

Books about Storytelling

Explore books related to storytelling. Refer to the following bibliography of related books. Can you list the reasons these writers feel (know) that storytelling is important? How do these authors approach the art of storytelling? What is the essence of each of the books you explore?

Baker, Augusta. 1977. *Storytelling: Art and Technique.* New York: R. R. Bowker.

Bauer, Caroline Feller. 1977. *Handbook for Storytellers.* Chicago: American Library.

Bettelheim, Bruno. 1976. *The Uses of Enchantment: The Meaning and Importance of Fairy Tales.* New York: Alfred A. Knopf.

Breneman, Lucille N., and Bren Breneman. 1984. *A Storytelling Handbook: Once upon a Time.* Chicago: Nelson-Hall.

Harrell, John. 1983. *Origins and Early Traditions of Storytelling.* Kensington, Calif.: York House.

Livo, Norma J., and Sandra A. Rietz. 1986. *Storytelling: Process and Practice.* Littleton, Colo.: Libraries Unlimited.

MacDonald, Margaret Read. 1982. *The Storyteller's Sourcebook: A Subject Title and Motif Index to Folklore Collections for Children*. Detroit, Mich.: Neal-Schuman.

Maguire, Jack. 1985. *Creative Storytelling*. New York: McGraw-Hill.

Morgan, John, and Mario Rinvolucri. 1983. *Once upon a Time: Using Stories in the Language Classroom*. New York: Cambridge University Press.

Pellowski, Anne. 1984. *The Story Vine*. New York: Macmillan.

_____. 1977. *The World of Storytelling*. New York: R. R. Bowker.

Ross, Ramon. 1980. *Storyteller*. Columbus, Ohio: Charles E. Merrill.

Sawyer, Ruth. 1942. *The Way of the Storyteller*. New York: Viking.

Schimmel, Nancy. 1978. *Just Enough to Make a Story*. Berkeley, Calif.: Sister's Choice.

Shedd, Charlie, and Martha Shedd. 1984. *Tell Me a Story*. Garden City, N.Y.: Doubleday.

Shedlock, Marie. 1951. *The Art of Storytelling*. New York: Dover.

Tooze, Ruth. 1959. *Storytelling*. Englewood Cliffs, N.J.: Prentice-Hall.

Yolen, Jane. 1981. *Touch Magic*. New York: Philomel.

Ziskind, Sylvia. 1976. *Telling Stories to Children*. Bronx, N.Y.: Wilson.